Ancient Science

40 Time-Traveling, World-Exploring, History-Making Activities for Kids

Jim Wiese

Illustrations by Ed Shems

JOSSEY-BASS
A Wiley Imprint
www.josseybass.com

For all the parents and
teachers who help make
science come alive

Published by Jossey-Bass
A Wiley Imprint
989 Market Street, San Francisco, CA 94103-1741   www.josseybass.com

Published simultaneously in Canada

Design and production by Navta Associates, Inc.

Jossey-Bass books and products are available through most bookstores. To contact Jossey-Bass
directly call our Customer Care Department within the U.S. at 800-956-7739, outside the U.S. at
317-572-3986, or fax 317-572-4002.

Jossey-Bass also publishes its books in a variety of electronic formats. Some content that appears in
print may not be available in electronic books.

Library of Congress Cataloging-in-Publication Data

Wiese, Jim, date.
    Ancient science : 40 time-traveling, world-exploring, history-making activities for kids
 / Jim Wiese.
      p. cm.
    Includes bibliographical references and index.
    ISBN 0-471-21595-3 (pbk. : acid-free paper)
    1. Science, Ancient—Study and teaching (Elementary) 2. Science—Study and teaching
(Elementary)—Activity programs. I. Title.

Q124.95 .W54 2003
372.3'5—dc21   2002032428

FIRST EDITION
PB Printing   10 9 8 7 6 5 4 3

Contents

Acknowledgments

When I went to George Washington High School in Denver, Colorado, I had the chance to fulfill my high school history requirements by taking a class called Ancient History. I was fascinated by the stories my teacher told me of the beginning of human history. I learned about past civilizations that gave us democracy, great cities, and many scientific achievements. Ancient civilizations also built monuments, explored new worlds, and gave us great leaders. I learned that what and who we are today is the result of a process that began thousands of years ago. It was that thought that started this book. The purpose of this book is to show how different civilizations contributed to the world we live in today, to show the connections between history and science. Through the activities and stories, I hope you, too, will see how these subjects are linked and appreciate the influence each has on the other.

Again, I would like to thank the team of people at John Wiley & Sons who worked to make this book a reality. I would especially like to acknowledge the support and work of my editor, Kate Bradford. Her professionalism in every aspect of the publishing process continues to bring out the best in my writing.

Introduction

*H*ave you ever wondered where paper came from? Or who made the first clock? Or who invented the compass or the magnifying glass? If you've ever asked yourself questions like these but don't know where to begin to find the answers, *Ancient Science* is the place to start. Science ideas have come from all over the world and from many different civilizations and cultures. Advances in science and technology have helped shape human history since ancient humans first learned to use tools, plant crops, and study the heavens.

Ancient Science lets you investigate some of the greatest scientific discoveries and the people who first introduced them to the world, from Egyptian clocks, Greek lighthouses, and Roman bridges to Chinese kites and Mesopotamian soap. So get ready for 40 exciting activities that will let you learn more about the people and cultures that helped make so many modern things (including books!) possible.

How to Use This Book

Every ancient civilization contributed something to science, so this book is divided into chapters based on civilization, including Egyptian, Roman, Greek, Mayan and Aztec, Chinese, Middle Eastern, and others. In each chapter there are groups of projects that teach you about some of the scientific contributions of each culture. Each project has a list of materials and a procedure to follow. You'll be able to find most of the materials needed around the house or at your neighborhood hardware or grocery store.

Some of the projects have a section called More Fun Stuff to Do that lets you try different variations on the original activity. Explanations are given at the end of each project. Words in **bold** type are defined in the glossary at the back of the book.

Being a Good Scientist

Read through the instructions once completely and collect all the equipment you'll need before you start the activity or experiment.

Keep a notebook. Write down what you do in each experiment or project and what happens.

Follow the instructions carefully. *Do not attempt to do by yourself any steps that require the help of an adult.*

If your project does not work properly the first time, try again or try doing it in a slightly different way. Experiments don't always work perfectly the first time.

Always have an open mind that asks questions and looks for answers. The basis of good science is asking good questions and finding the best answers.

Increasing Your Understanding

Make small changes in the design of the equipment or project to see if the results stay the same. Change only one thing at a time so you can tell which change caused a particular result.

Make up an experiment or activity to test your own ideas about how things work.

Look at the world around you for examples of the scientific principles that you have learned.

Don't worry if at first you don't understand how everything works. There will always be new things to discover. Remember that many of the most famous discoveries were made by accident.

Using This Book to Do a Science Fair Project

Many of the activities in this book can serve as the starting point for a science fair project. After doing the experiment as it is written in the book, what questions come to mind? Some possible projects are suggested in the section of the activities called More Fun Stuff to Do.

To begin your science fair project, first write down the problem you want to study and come up with a hypothesis. A **hypothesis** is an educated guess about the results of an experiment you are going to perform. For example, if you enjoyed doing the Pyramid Power activity, you may want to find out how other inclined planes work to complete a task. A hypothesis for this experiment could be that a longer inclined plane makes it easier to move the block up the ramp.

Next you will have to devise an experiment to test your hypothesis. In the Pyramid Power example, you might test several inclined planes of different lengths, then observe and record the results as the block moves up the ramp. Be sure to keep careful records of your experiment. Next analyze the data you recorded. In the Pyramid Power example, you could create a table showing the length of the inclined plane and the force necessary to move the block, and then you could graph the results. Finally, come up with a conclusion that shows how your results prove or disprove your hypothesis.

This process is called the **scientific method.** When following the scientific method, you begin with a hypothesis, test it with an experiment, analyze the results, and draw a conclusion.

A Word of Warning

Some science experiments can be dangerous. *Ask an adult to help you with experiments that call for adult help, such as those that involve matches, knives, or other dangerous materials.* Don't forget to ask your parents' permission to use household items, and put away your equipment and clean up your work area when you have finished experimenting. Good scientists are careful and avoid accidents.

SCIENCE FROM THE DAWN OF TIME

The First Humans

Every civilization has contributed to the scientific knowledge that we use today. Some early civilizations such as the ancient Egyptians, Greeks, Chinese, and Romans lasted longer than others and left many records, so we know more about them. But others, such as the earliest known societies in Africa, India, and Europe, left few records. We have to try and interpret what these cultures knew from the things they left behind.

An **archaeologist** is a scientist who studies the remains of past peoples. Archeologists dig up ancient **fossils** (bones that have been turned to stone) and **artifacts** (objects made by humans, such as primitive tools, weapons, cooking pots, or works of art). They then study these artifacts to determine when humans first used fire, when they made their first stone tools, the types of crops they first cultivated, and so on. The oldest artifacts have been found in an area known as the Olduvai Gorge in Tanzania, Africa.

To learn more about some of the earliest humans and their discoveries, try the activities in this chapter.

PROJECT

1

The Stone Age

It's thought that the first humanoid apes walked the plains of west and south Africa over 4 million years ago. But the first stone tools didn't appear until about 2.4 million years ago. These first crude stone tools were used for scraping and hammering, and they marked our departure from other species of animals. Simple stone tools were the technology that first made us human. Try this activity to learn the science behind how simple tools make work easier.

Materials

1-yard (1-m) piece of ½-inch-
   (1.25-cm) diameter dowel
felt marker

sharp knife
adult helper

Procedure

1. Take the dowel outside to a lawn area.

2. Stick one end of the dowel into the ground. How hard is it to push the dowel into the ground? Use the marker to mark on the dowel the depth the dowel goes into the ground. How deep does the dowel go?

3. Have the adult use the knife to sharpen one end of the dowel into a point.

4. Stick the pointed end of the dowel into the ground near where you previously stuck the dowel. How hard is it to push in this time? Again, mark the depth the dowel goes into the ground. How deep does the dowel go?

More Fun Stuff to Do

Find a pile of rocks outside that you can examine. A good place to search is near a rocky shore by a lake or a river. Look through the rocks. Can you find a rock that is smooth and about the size of your fist? What tool could that become? Can you find a rock that has been broken and has one sharp edge? What tool could that become? Can you find any other rocks that might be used as tools? How could you break a rock if you wanted to make it a different shape?

Explanation

The dowel with the pointed end goes deeper into the ground than the dowel with a flat end, and it's easier to push. It may seem simple, but the tool you made in this activity actually took early humans thousands of years to figure out. When a dowel or a stick is sharpened, it becomes a digging tool or a spear. Rocks that have certain shapes, like the kind you found in More Fun Stuff to Do, can be used as hammers, knives, scrapers, or ax heads.

A sharpened object is an example of a simple machine called a wedge. Many archaeologists believe that the wedge was the first simple machine discovered by early humans. A wedge makes work easier because it causes force to be concentrated in a smaller area. When you push the dowel without a point into the ground, the force of your push is spread out over the entire end of the dowel. But when you sharpen the dowel, the same force is concentrated at the point of the dowel, making it easier to stick in the ground. When digging up edible roots for an ancient dinner, a pointed stick could save time and energy that would otherwise be expended scraping and grubbing with flat stones or fingers.

Ancient Science in Action

During Paleolithic times, or the Old Stone Age, the first stone tools were crude fist-size wedges made by splitting one stone with another. These first tools were probably used to cut up and chop plant and animal materials, as well as for digging. Sharpened stone tools, called hand axes, date back to about 1.3 million years ago. Hand axes were used for cutting, scraping, digging, and probably killing. At the beginning of Neolithic times, or the New Stone Age, stone tools were made smoother by polishing the sharp edges with sand.

By the end of Neolithic times, stone tools were being used to make other tools out of softer materials, such as wood and antlers. Late Neolithic humans made sewing needles and fishhooks out of antlers.

PROJECT 2

Make It Grow

*H*umans in the Old Stone Age were nomadic, meaning they moved in groups from place to place, taking everything they owned with them. They were hunters and gatherers, which means they hunted animals and gathered plants and fruit for food. But around 10,000 B.C.E. some early humans began to settle in communities that revolved around agriculture, cultivating plants and raising animals. To supply food for the people in the community, they began to grow their own plants rather than just eating the ones that they found in nature. But there is more to growing plants than just throwing a few seeds on the ground, as the humans in the first agricultural communities no doubt understood. Try this activity to investigate the conditions needed to cultivate plants.

Materials

2 plastic cups   millet seeds (available from a pet store)
potting soil   water
sand   paper
felt marker   pencil

Procedure

1. Fill one of the plastic cups halfway with soil and the other cup halfway with sand. Use the felt marker to label the outside of each cup "soil" or "sand."

2. Sprinkle several millet seeds in each cup.

3. Cover the seeds in the soil cup with a thin layer of soil, and the seeds in the sand cup with a thin layer of sand.

4. Water the soil and sand until they're just damp.

5. Place the plastic cups on a windowsill so that they get sunlight.

6. Water the seeds every other day.

7. Observe and record what you see happening to the seeds every day.

Explanation

The seeds in both cups should sprout and begin to grow in a short time. However, the millet seeds will grow better in soil than in sand.

Most plants require sunlight, water, and nutrients in order to grow. Green plants use water and minerals in the soil, carbon dioxide from the air, and sunlight to make glucose in a process called **photosynthesis.** Sand has few minerals in it, so it is not good for growing plants.

The first humans settled in the Indus Valley between modern India and Pakistan, the area between the Tigris and Euphrates rivers in modern Iraq, the Yellow River valley in China, and the Nile River valley in northeastern Africa. These are all areas with good soil, plenty of water, and a lot of sun. In these regions, large nearby rivers would flood every spring, depositing a rich silt that turned desert into farmlands. The river also gave a supply of fish and water birds to eat, as well as mud to build shelters.

Millet, which you grew here, and other cereal crops such as wheat, barley, and sorghum, were the first plants to be grown by early humans in the Nubian Desert of northeastern Sudan, in Africa. Along with the cultivation of crops, early humans also domesticated animals, such as sheep and goats.

Ancient Science in Action

Because early humans could now stay in one place for a longer period of time, they began to make more permanent structures of mud and brick, and towns and villages were born. Growing crops and domesticating animals meant more food, which allowed the populations to rapidly increase. It also meant that new implements, such as stones for grinding and pots for storage, were needed to manage the supplies. And it also led to trade between communities, as food surpluses could be exchanged for other kinds of food. For example, surplus millet grown near the Nile River could be traded for wild honey from mountain communities. As communities grew, civilizations were born.

PROJECT 3

Sweet Tooth

While early humans were growing cereal grains in Africa, early humans in other areas were raising other types of plants. Around 3000 B.C.E., an early civilization centered in the Indus Valley (along the border between modern India and Pakistan) began to grow plants that were found in their region, such as einkorn (a wild form of wheat), barley, and date palms.

In 327 B.C.E. Alexander the Great, the king of Macedonia and conqueror of much of Asia, reported that a plant he had never seen grew in the Indus Valley near modern-day India. We now know that this plant was sugarcane. Sugar was first removed from the cane by chewing and sucking the stalk of the sugarcane plant. But by 300 C.E., people in India had developed a process in which sugar syrup could be extracted by boiling and pressing the canes. Once sugar syrup was made, it wouldn't have been long before people noticed what happened when sugar syrup hardened. Try this activity to find out how to turn sugar syrup into sugar crystals.

Materials

drinking glass   scissors
water   pencil
saucepan   paper clip
spoon   paper towel
sugar   adult helper
string

Procedure

1. Fill the drinking glass about one-third full of water. Empty the water into the saucepan.

2. Have your adult helper heat the water to boiling, then remove the pan from the heat.

3. Use the spoon to stir sugar into the water until no more sugar will dissolve. *(Note: You can dissolve a lot of sugar in the water, about two times as much as the amount of water you started with.)* You should end with a thick syrup that has a few grains of undissolved sugar floating in it.

4. Pour the sugar syrup into the drinking glass.

5. Cut a piece of string so that it is slightly longer than the drinking glass is tall.

6. Tie one end of the string to the pencil and the other end to the paper clip.

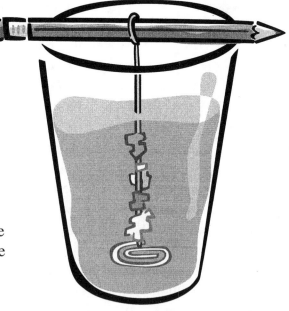

7. Wet the string and paper clip with water, then roll them through some dry sugar so that a few sugar crystals stick to them.

8. Place the pencil across the rim of the glass so that the string and paper clip are suspended in the syrup solution.

9. Place the glass where it won't be disturbed and cover it with a paper towel to keep dust and dirt out of the solution.

10. After about five days, observe the string. What has happened?

11. Take the string and sugar crystals out of the solution and taste the crystals. What do they taste like?

More Fun Stuff to Do

Pour some sugar on a piece of paper and observe it with a magnifying glass. What does it look like? How does it compare to the sugar that forms on the string? Can you think why?

Explanation

After several days, sugar crystals will begin to form on the string and paper clip. If the water evaporates slowly, the crystals will become quite large. The crystals will taste sweet. If you do the More Fun Stuff to Do activity, the sugar will look like small crystals through the magnifying glass. These crystals look like smaller versions of the large crystals that formed on the string and paper clip.

When sugar is dissolved in water, it becomes a sugar solution. In a solution, one substance is completely dissolved into another. To get

ANCIENT SCIENCE IN ACTION

Sugarcane isn't the only plant that sugar comes from. Native Americans found out that the sap of maple trees could be boiled to make maple sugar syrup. No one knows how long they had been doing this, but the practice was probably well established before Columbus introduced the sugarcane plant to the West Indies. Sugar also comes from sugar beets, a fact that was discovered in Germany in the 18th century.

the sugar out of the solution, all you have to do is let the water slowly evaporate. When that happens, sugar crystals are left behind. A **crystal** is a chemical compound that forms a solid in a specific pattern that repeats regularly in all directions. Only certain chemicals, such as sugar and salt, will form crystals. Crystals can form cubes, diamonds, pyramids, and other regular shapes.

Sky Sign

People have been navigating (steering a course) on rivers, lakes, and oceans since long before recorded history. Archaeological discoveries show that the Vikings and the Polynesians made epic voyages long before the invention of the magnetic compass. They left no record of how they accomplished these feats, but they probably used their knowledge of prevailing winds and the positions of the sun and stars to determine direction. One very important star in navigation is Polaris, also called the North Star. It can always be seen on a clear night in the northern sky of Earth's northern hemisphere, so if you stand facing it, you know you're facing north. Try the following activity to learn how to find the North Star.

Materials

directional compass

Note: This activity should be done outdoors on a clear night.

Procedure

1. Lay the compass flat in your hand, allowing the needle to spin freely. When the needle has stopped, it will be pointing north. Look in that direction.

2. Look at the northern part of the sky and locate the Big Dipper. The Big Dipper is a group of seven stars that looks like a ladle. Three stars make a curved handle, and four stars make the ladle's bowl.

3. Find the two stars on the outside part of the Big Dipper's bowl. Follow these two pointer stars to a star of average brightness. This is Polaris, the North Star.

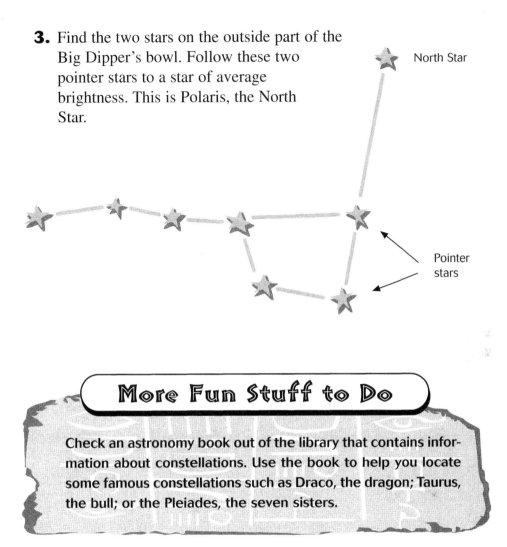

North Star

Pointer stars

More Fun Stuff to Do

Check an astronomy book out of the library that contains information about constellations. Use the book to help you locate some famous constellations such as Draco, the dragon; Taurus, the bull; or the Pleiades, the seven sisters.

Explanation

When you look at the northern sky on a clear night, you should be able to locate the North Star. With practice, you will be able to locate many constellations as well.

Because the Earth spins on its axis, the North Pole always points in the same direction. Polaris is called the North Star because it is located almost directly above the North Pole. For years, people used the North Star and other constellations to navigate.

If you watch the stars for many nights, you will see that the whole dome of the sky seems to move from east to west. But the sky dome isn't actually moving. The spinning of the Earth on its axis causes the stars to appear to move. Because the stars are so far away, they appear to move as a group, always keeping the same relative position in relation to each other. Stars do move, but so slowly that it takes thousands of years before there are any visible changes in the night sky.

Ancient Science in Action

Early mariners (people who traveled on water) didn't travel very far from the coast. They usually followed the coastlines, where they knew the position of their ships by identifying objects on land. They would travel during the day and go ashore at night. After they learned to use the stars to navigate, sailors began to travel at night as well, increasing the distance they could go.

There have been many ancient peoples who have studied the stars for navigation. The people living near the Mediterranean Sea—the Sumerians, Cretans, Egyptians, Phoenicians, and Greeks—became gifted seamen, as did the Scandinavians in northern Europe and the South Pacific's Polynesians.

PROJECT 5

Pop Music

Archaeologists have discovered what may have been one of the first musical instruments, a hollow bone used as a whistle. The first horns and pipes were made in prehistoric times from natural substances such as bone, horn, wood, and reeds. Drums also date back to prehistoric times, and probably began as hollow logs that people banged on. Stringed instruments began to appear around 2500 B.C.E. Music seems to have always been a part of our lives. But how did the earliest instruments, like the whistle and drum, make different sounds? Try this activity to find out how they make different sounds.

Materials

6 empty glass pop bottles, the same size and shape

paper

pencil

water

Procedure

1. Line up the bottles on the table and label them from 1 to 6, using the paper and pencil.

2. Pour water into the first bottle to a level of about 1 inch (2.5 cm).

3. In the second bottle, pour water so that it is about 1 inch (2.5 cm) higher than the first, to a level of 2 inches (5 cm).

4. Pour water into each of the next bottles so that it is about 1 inch (2.5 cm) higher than in the previous bottle. This will give you 6 bottles, each with a different amount of water.

5. Use the pencil to gently tap the sides of the first bottle. What happens? Try tapping the rest of the bottles.

6. Now blow across the top of each bottle in order. What happens?

More Fun Stuff to Do

You can change the sound each bottle makes by adding or removing water. Add different amounts of water to make your bottles play different notes. Can you play a song on your bottles?

Explanation

When you strike the bottles or blow across their mouths, they will make different sounds. The relative highness or lowness of a sound is called the sound's **pitch.** When you hit the bottles, the bottle with little water in it will make a sound that's a higher pitch, while the bottle with more water in it will make a sound that's a lower pitch. When you blow into the bottle with little water in it, it will give a sound with a lower pitch, while the bottle with more water in it will make a sound that's a higher pitch.

All sounds are produced by the vibrations of a material. As the material vibrates, it causes the air around it to vibrate as well. When the vibrating air hits your eardrum, you perceive it as sound. In this activity, the difference in the pitch of the sound that results from whether you hit the bottle or blew on its mouth is the result of what was vibrating, the water in the bottle or the air above it.

Percussion instruments are instruments that make a sound when you hit them, such as the drum, xylophone, triangle, and cymbal. Hitting the instrument causes it to vibrate, and these vibrations reach your ears as sounds. The different sounds made by different percussion instruments are created by the different materials, the different sizes, and the different shapes of the instruments. In this activity, when you hit the bottle, it acts like a percussion instrument. The hit causes both the bottle and the water to vibrate. If there is just a little water in the bottle, the vibrations are faster, and the pitch is higher. When there is more water in the bottle, the vibrations are slower, and the pitch is lower.

Wind instruments are instruments that make a sound when you blow air into them, such as the flute, trumpet, horn, and clarinet. Blowing into these instruments causes the air inside them to vibrate. In this activity, when you blew into the bottle, the air vibrated. In the wind instruments, a short column of air produces a higher pitch, and a long column of air produces a lower pitch. When you blew across the mouth of the bottle with a lot of water, the column of air was shorter, so you produced a higher-pitched sound. When you blew across the bottle with very little water, the column of air was longer, so you produced a lower-pitched sound.

SCIENCE FROM THE FERTILE CRESCENT

Ancient Mesopotamia

A crescent-shaped area between two great rivers, the Tigris and the Euphrates, in a part of what we now call the Middle East was the site of one of the world's first civilizations. Because the water from the two rivers made it especially good for growing plants, this region later became known as the Fertile Crescent. By 3500 B.C.E., the first cities had already grown up in this region, also known as Mesopotamia, which was home to the ancient Sumerians, Babylonians, Phoenicians, and some Semitic tribes, among others.

The people of Mesopotamia invented the wheel and the axle and used the first wheeled cart. The Mesopotamians also invented soap and metal coins.

To learn more about what this region contributed to the world, try the activities in this chapter.

PROJECT 1

Scrubbing Bubbles

The origin of the first soap is still a bit of a mystery, but archaeologists discovered a Mesopotamian recipe for soap inscribed on clay pots dating from about 2800 B.C.E. The recipe described a cleaning solution made from 1 part oil and $5\frac{1}{2}$ parts potash (a chemical compound obtained from boiling wood ash). Try this activity to learn how soap works.

Materials

jar with screw-top lid
cold water
measuring spoon

vegetable oil
dishwashing soap

Procedure

1. Fill the jar half full of cold water.

2. Measure one teaspoon (5 ml) of vegetable oil and pour it into the jar. What does the oil do when poured onto the water?

3. Screw the lid tightly on the jar. Shake the jar to mix the water and oil solution.

4. Set the jar on the table and observe. What happens?

5. Remove the jar lid and add 1 tablespoon (15 ml) of dishwashing soap to the jar.

6. Again screw the lid tightly on the jar and shake it to mix the water, oil, and soap.

7. Set the jar on the table and observe. What happens?

More Fun Stuff to Do

Try the experiment again, only this time use warm water. How does the use of warm water affect the results of your experiment?

Explanation

When you add oil to water, the oil will sit on the surface of the water. When you shake the solution, the oil and water will initially mix, but after you set the jar on the table, the oil and water will again separate. When you add soap to the water and oil and shake the jar, the oil will mix with the water again, but this time, after you set the jar on the table, most of the oil and water will not separate. In More Fun Stuff to Do, when you repeat the experiment with warm water, more oil stays suspended in the water.

Soap is made by mixing fats and oils with a strong alkali compound such as potash or lye. An alkali substance is a base, a chemical that reacts with an acid to form a salt and water. The molecules that make up soap are very unusual. One end of a soap molecule is usually made of either sodium or potassium (which comes from the alkali compound). This end of the molecule is **hydrophilic,** which means it is attracted to water but repels oils. The other end of the molecule is a long chain of atoms called triglycerides (which come from the fat and oils). This end is **hydrophobic,** which means that it will repel water but is attracted to oily substances.

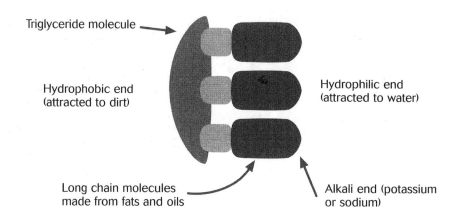

Triglyceride molecule

Hydrophobic end
(attracted to dirt)

Hydrophilic end
(attracted to water)

Long chain molecules
made from fats and oils

Alkali end (potassium
or sodium)

In this activity, you saw the effect that a soap molecule has on an oil molecule. When the soap molecule is mixed with water, it moves to the surface. The sodium end stays in the water, while the oil end sticks up in the air. When dirt, oil, and grease come in contact with soap, such as when your dirty clothes are put in soapy water, they are attracted to the hydrophobic end of the molecule. When the soapy water is moved around, the hydrophilic end of the soap molecule is pulled around with the water. This hydrophilic end pulls the rest of the molecule with it. Since the hydrophobic end is still stuck to the dirt, the dirt is pulled out of the clothes and they become clean. Rinsing in clean water washes any remaining soap out of the clothes.

The reaction of soap and dirt is affected by temperature. When a solution is warmed, the molecules in it move faster. As the molecules move faster, they make more collisions with other molecules. As the molecules collide with each other, the speed of the chemical reaction increases. If a solution is cooled, the molecules in it move more slowly and collide with fewer other molecules, and the speed of the reaction decreases. In this activity, the reaction between soap and dirt happens faster in warm water and slower in cold water, as you saw in More Fun Stuff to Do.

ANCIENT SCIENCE IN ACTION

Records show that the ancient Egyptians washed regularly in a solution made from scented oils and potash. The Greeks and the Romans made their soap from olive oil and pumice powder (a volcanic rock). After the fall of the Roman Empire in 467, there was a decline in bathing and the use of soap in Europe until the 17th century.

PROJECT 2

Free Wheeling

It is generally recognized that the wheel was first introduced by the Sumerians around 3200 B.C.E. Wheels were actually already in use for making pottery (potters shape clay on a wheel that can be easily turned), but it was the Sumerians who first used wheels on vehicles. Sumerian carts had heavy, solid wooden wheels made from two or three planks fastened together and cut into a disc. These wheels rotated around a hole in their center that was placed on a fixed axle (a fixed axle turns with the wheel). These carts were pulled by oxen and donkeys. Try this activity to learn about how the wheel and the axle make work easier.

Materials

metal hook with screw on one end
2-by-4-by-6-inch (5-by-10-by-15-cm) block of wood
spring scale (available in hardware and sporting goods stores)
paper
pencil
15 plastic drinking straws

2-inch- (5-cm) diameter jar lid
thick cardboard
scissors
tape
two 6-inch (15-cm) pieces of wire
glue

Procedure

1. Screw the metal hook into one end of the block. Link one end of the spring scale through the hook.

2. With the wooden block flat on the table, pull the other end of the spring scale, moving the block along the table. Measure the force needed to move the block by reading the value from the spring scale and record the result.

3. Set one straw aside to use in Step 6. Spread the remaining straws on the table parallel to one another and about $\frac{1}{4}$ to $\frac{1}{2}$ inch (.625 to 1.25 cm) apart.

4. Place the wooden block on the straws near one side of the straws. Again pull the other end of the spring scale to move the block across the straws. Measure and record the force needed to move the block this time.

5. Use the jar lid to trace four 2-inch (5-cm) circles on the cardboard. Use the scissors to cut them out.

6. Cut one plastic straw in half. Tape each half-straw to the bottom of the wooden block, one near each end of the block.

7. Insert one piece of wire through each straw. These will be the axles for your vehicle.

8. Push the center of one cardboard wheel onto each wire end. Add glue to hold the cardboard wheels to the axles.

9. With the wooden vehicle on the table, pull the other end of the spring scale, moving the block along the table. Measure and record the force needed to move the block. With which method is it easiest to move the wooden block?

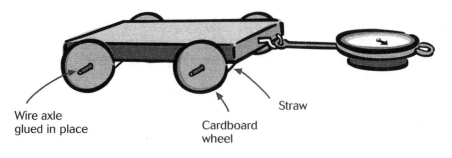

Wire axle
glued in place

Cardboard
wheel

Straw

Explanation

It will take the most force to slide the wooden block across the table. Although rolling the block on the plastic straws takes less force, the block quickly reaches the end of the straws, and the straws would have to be moved in order to move the block farther. As a wheel-and-axle vehicle, the block will be the easiest to move.

The wooden vehicle you made in the last part of this project moves easily because it has round cardboard wheels with a wire axle. This forms a simple machine called the wheel and axle. A wheel will roll and move an object more easily than just dragging the object because it creates less **friction,** the force that opposes motion.

Few inventions have been more important, or have more obscure origins, than the wheel. One theory is that early humans first discovered that a large, heavy object could be moved more easily if it was rolled on round logs rather than slid along the ground. Someone then figured out that a round piece of log (the wheel) could be rotated on a smaller stick (the axle). This wheel was first used horizontally as a potter's wheel, where it could be easily spun around to aid in shaping clay pots. Later someone put wheels on both ends of the axle and added a cart body, and the first wheeled vehicle was invented.

Ancient Science in Action

By 2000 B.C.E., lighter-spoked wheels were developed and used on faster-wheeled vehicles, such as the chariot. In a spoked wheel, the wheel is not solid but uses braces or bars extending from the hub to the rim of the wheel. This makes the wheels lighter and easier to turn. Copper rims were added to the outside of the wheels to increase their strength. Between 265 and 221 B.C.E., the Chinese invented the wheelbarrow. This large handcart enabled a single person to transport a heavy load. The Chinese name for the wheelbarrow is "wooden ox."

Where in the World

The first known maps appear on clay tablets from Babylonia that date back to at least 2500 B.C.E. These maps use symbols and writing to identify features such as mountains and rivers, buildings, and compass directions. Try this activity to learn how to make a map of your own neighborhood.

Materials

paper   magnetic compass
number 2 pencil   colored pencils

Note: This activity should be done in your own home.

Procedure

1. Lay the paper flat on the table. Draw a double black line down the middle of it to represent the street you live on.

2. Turn the paper so that the line on the paper runs parallel to your actual street. (This will help you map your neighborhood more easily.)

3. Place the magnetic compass on the paper. Draw an arrow in the top right corner of the paper that points to the direction the compass shows as north.

4. Draw a square next to the street line showing where your house is located. (Make sure you draw it on the correct side of the line.)

5. Add nearby streets to your map by drawing more black lines. Label the streets. Think about making the lines closer or farther away, depending on how close or far away the streets actually are.

6. Draw and label any bodies of water, such as creeks, streams, or rivers, that are near your house, using a blue pencil.

7. Draw and label any other large areas, such as parks, woods, hills, or fields, using a green pencil.

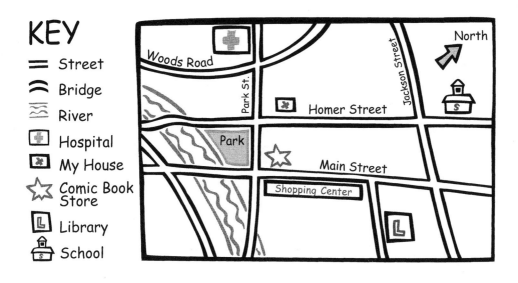

KEY

= Street
≈ Bridge
≈ River
⊞ Hospital
⊠ My House
☆ Comic Book Store
Ⓛ Library
🏫 School

8. Outline any easily recognized structures, such as schools, libraries, or large office buildings. Think of symbols and colors that you can use on your map to represent the different types of buildings. For example, a hospital might be represented by a red cross, or a school by a square with an "S" on it. Add these symbols to the map. Write what these symbols mean as a "key" to your map. Put the key in a blank corner of the map if there's room.

9. Finally, add other places you think are important. For example, draw in your friends' houses, local stores, and so on.

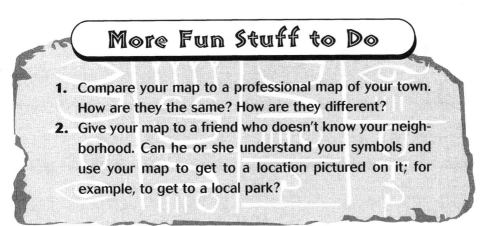

More Fun Stuff to Do

1. Compare your map to a professional map of your town. How are they the same? How are they different?

2. Give your map to a friend who doesn't know your neighborhood. Can he or she understand your symbols and use your map to get to a location pictured on it; for example, to get to a local park?

Explanation

You should be able to make a simple map of your neighborhood. It will be similar to a professional town map but will probably contain less detail. However, a friend should be able to use it to get around your neighborhood.

The oldest recorded map is a representation of a town found in a wall painting in Anatolia (Turkey) that dates to 6100 B.C.E. The map shows a town plan with about 80 buildings. In the background is a drawing of a volcano that looks like it is erupting.

ANCIENT SCIENCE IN ACTION

The ancient Greeks added horizontal and vertical lines to their maps. These lines were developed into the latitude and longitude lines that we see on modern maps. The first map of the world was compiled by Anaximander from Miletus in the early 6th century B.C.E.

The ancient Romans improved on map techniques by producing road maps with towns and cities clearly marked. This made travel between cities much easier.

PROJECT 4

Money, Money, Money

No one knows when people first started using objects such as shells, stones, and animal bones as money. The first metallic money appears to have been small bronze pieces used in Mesopotamia. The earliest coins came from Lydia (modern western Turkey) and were made from **electrum,** a natural **alloy** (mixture) of gold and silver. Each coin was heated to make it malleable (able to easily change shape), placed between engraved dies, and then struck with a hammer. The dies had different symbols or pictures on them, which were engraved on the coin by the process. Coins of pure silver and gold were created by

King Croesus in 561 B.C.E. Today, most coins are made of different metals, such as iron, nickel, and zinc. How can you determine if a coin is made of certain metals? Try this activity to find out.

Materials

U.S. coins (penny, nickel, dime, and quarter)
Canadian coins (penny, nickel, dime, and quarter)
bar magnet

Procedure

1. Place the U.S. coins on the table. Next to each U.S. coin, place the Canadian coin of the same value.

2. Observe each pair of coins. How are they the same? How are they different?

3. Take the magnet and touch each of the U.S. coins. What happens?

4. Take the magnet and touch each of the Canadian coins. What happens this time?

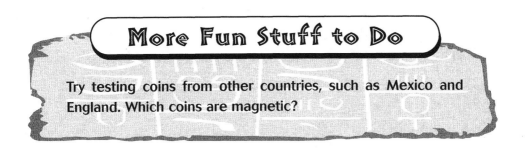

More Fun Stuff to Do

Try testing coins from other countries, such as Mexico and England. Which coins are magnetic?

Explanation

While the coins of the United States and Canada look similar, several Canadian coins—the nickel, dime, and quarter—are magnetic, while the same coins from the United States are not.

Magnetism is an invisible force that will attract certain metals to magnets. Coins are made of many different metals, such as copper, zinc, iron, and nickel. But only some metals are attracted to a magnet. Iron, nickel, and cobalt are attracted to a magnet, while copper and other metals are not. This means that copper pennies from both Canada and the United States are not attracted to a magnet. While you would think the nickel from the United States would be attracted to a magnet, only the Canadian nickel actually contains a large enough amount of the metal nickel to make the coin magnetic.

In 1982, there was a major change in the metal content of U.S. coins. The U.S. penny is now made of copper-plated zinc, and the U.S. nickel is an alloy of 75% copper and only 25% nickel. The U.S. dime, quarter, and half-dollar are all "clad" coins, produced from three metal strips that are bonded together and rolled to the required thickness. The face of these coins is 75% copper and 25% nickel, and the core, visible along the edges of the coins, is pure copper. Canadian dimes and quarters use more iron and nickel alloys (metal mixtures that contain nickel), so they are magnetic as well.

ANCIENT SCIENCE IN ACTION

In Greece, the engraving of coins became an art form. In 525 B.C.E., Darius I became the first ruler to collect taxes in coinage instead of goods from the people he ruled. When Alexander the Great conquered the known world, beginning in 336 B.C.E. when he became king, he began the practice of putting the faces of world rulers on coins so that their features would be recorded for posterity.

SCIENCE AMONG THE PYRAMIDS

Ancient Egypt

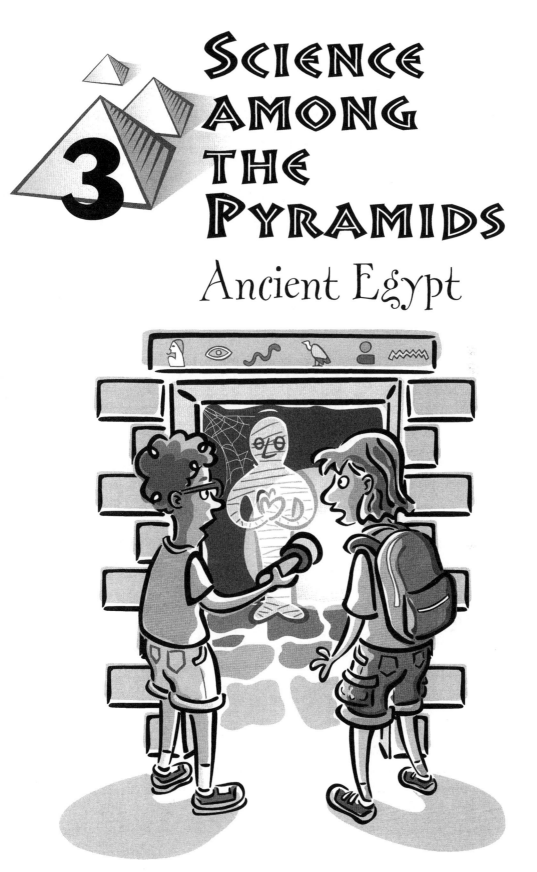

The Nile River valley in northern Africa had already been settled for centuries before the states of Upper and Lower Egypt were united under one king around 3000 B.C.E. to form what we now think of as ancient Egypt. The Egyptians had a thriving and distinctive culture until 30 B.C.E., when they were swallowed up by the Roman Empire.

The ancient Egyptians felt that they were the special favorites of the gods because they lived in such a wonderful land. Every year the Nile River flooded and deposited rich soil that turned the desert into farmland. The river also provided transportation and food. Along its banks grew a plant called papyrus, which the Egyptians beat flat so they could write on it as if it were paper. Beyond this fertile valley were deserts that kept invaders away, and that were also rich in natural resources such as gold and copper, and stones for building and for making jewelry.

Egyptian scientists studied **astronomy** (the study of the sun and stars). Through their practice of mummification they learned about the internal organs and systems of the human body. They also developed hieroglyphics, one of the earliest written languages.

To learn more about the ancient Egyptians and the science they studied, try the activities in this chapter.

PROJECT 1

Sticking Together

Glue is something we use all the time. But did you know that it was discovered thousands of years ago? Although no one knows who first discovered glue, the ancient Egyptians were known to have made glue by boiling together animal skin, bone, tendon, and ligaments. The goo that resulted when the water was boiled off was used to stick things like cloth and papyrus together. Even a casket removed from the tomb of King Tut shows the use of glue in its construction. Try the following activity to make some glue for yourself.

Materials

measuring cup

milk

measuring spoons

vinegar

saucepan

stove

mixing spoon

paper towel

strainer

plastic bowl

baking soda

water

paper

adult helper

Procedure

1. Place half a cup (125 ml) of milk and 1 tablespoon (15 ml) of vinegar in the pan. Have your adult helper gently warm the mixture on the stove while you stir occasionally with the spoon. The milk will turn into two substances: curds, the solid part, and whey, the liquid part.

2. Place a paper towel in the strainer. Hold the strainer over the plastic bowl and have your helper pour the mixture through the strainer. The whey will flow through the strainer into the bowl, while the curds will remain in the strainer.

3. Pour the curds from the strainer back into the pan and add $\frac{1}{4}$ teaspoon (1 ml) of baking soda. Stir gently. Don't be surprised if the baking soda reacts with any leftover vinegar by bubbling.

4. Slowly add water, a small amount at a time, to the mixture until the resulting glue is the right consistency for your use.

5. Test your glue by pasting two pieces of paper together.

Explanation

Your glue should be able to hold two pieces of paper together.

This project is an example of a chemical reaction. In a chemical reaction there is a change in matter in which substances break apart to produce one or more new substances. In this activity, you combine two substances, milk and vinegar, to make a new substance, glue. First you use the vinegar, an acid, to sour the milk. The milk breaks down into two new substances, the curds and whey. The curds are made of a protein found in milk called casein. When you add baking soda to the curds, you create another chemical reaction. This reaction between the protein, the baking soda, and any remaining vinegar results in another new substance, casein glue, a sticky protein.

The Egyptian animal glue was made using the proteins extracted from the bones, hides, hoofs, and horns of animals by boiling. The extract was then cooked to form a goo. The goo was heated when it was to be used, spread on objects like pieces of wood or paper, and then the objects were held together and allowed to dry. The objects were then stuck together.

ANCIENT SCIENCE IN ACTION

In addition to using glue on wood and papyrus, there is evidence that the Egyptians made the first adhesive bandage. Ancient records mention simple medications spread on cloth that was wrapped around a wound, then held in place with glue.

PROJECT 2

Pyramid Power

The Egyptian pyramids are still some of the most amazing structures in the world. People have often wondered how the ancient Egyptians were able to build the pyramids. They had to lift large blocks of stone higher and higher as the pyramids grew taller. How did they do it? Try this activity to learn one way they probably made their task easier.

Materials

metal hook with a screw at one end
block of wood
spring scale (available from most hardware or sporting goods stores)

paper
pencil
smooth board for a ramp
several books

Procedure

1. Screw the hook into one end of the block of wood.

2. Hook the block to the end of the spring scale. Use the spring scale to lift the block straight up. Record the force of gravity exerted on the block by reading the weight on the scale.

3. Use books to prop up one end of the board so that the books are about one-third as high as the length of the board.

4. Use the spring scale to pull the block up the ramp at a steady speed. Record the force needed to pull the block this way.

5. Which way took less force to move the block, lifting it straight up or pulling it up the ramp?

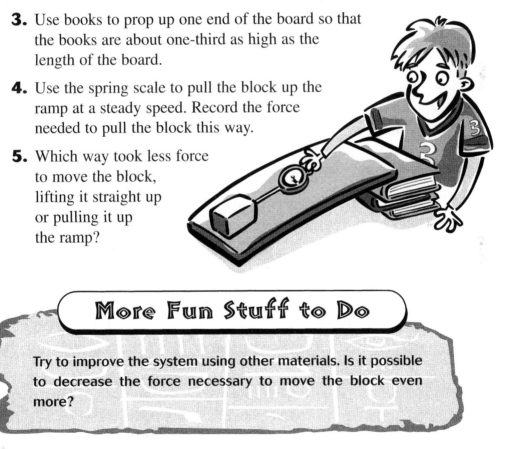

More Fun Stuff to Do

Try to improve the system using other materials. Is it possible to decrease the force necessary to move the block even more?

Explanation

It will take less force to pull the block up the ramp than to lift it straight up.

In this activity, you used a simple machine, a device that helps people do work more easily, the ramp, to make it easier to move the block to the top of the pile of books. The ramp is actually a simple machine called an "inclined plane." All machines, no matter how complex, are made up of one or more of the six simple machines: the inclined plane, the wedge, the screw, the lever, the wheel and axle, and the pulley.

Every machine performs at least one of the following functions:

1. A machine may transfer forces from one place to another. For example, the chain of a bicycle transfers the force from the pedals to the rear wheel.

2. A machine may change the direction of a force. For example, a rope thrown over a tree branch can be used to lift a box. The box is lifted up by you pulling down on the opposite end of the rope.

3. A machine may multiply speed or distance.

4. A machine may multiply force.

The amount by which a machine can multiply a force is called **mechanical advantage.** You can calculate the mechanical advantage of any machine by using the following equation:

$$\text{mechanical advantage} = \frac{\text{load force}}{\text{effort force}}$$

Load force is the force needed to move the object without the machine, and effort force is the force needed to move the object with the machine.

For example, the effort force required to push a person in a wheel-chair up a ramp is 100 N. (*N* is short for Newton. One Newton is approximately the force needed to lift .1 kg [.22 pounds] against gravity.) If the person and the wheelchair had to be lifted straight up against gravity, the load force would be 900 N. You can calculate the mechanical advantage by using the equation:

$$\text{mechanical advantage} = \frac{\text{load force}}{\text{effort force}}$$

$$= \frac{900 \text{ N}}{100 \text{ N}}$$

$$= 9$$

This means that the ramp multiplies the effort force by nine times. However, even though you only need one-ninth the force to move the wheelchair, you have to push it nine times as far. The net result will be that the same amount of work will be done. Simple machines will make the tradeoff of a decreased effort for an increased distance in order to accomplish a task. In both cases however, the same amount of work is done.

With a ramp with an incline of 30 degrees, it should take about half the force to slide the block up the ramp that it took to lift it. This would give your ramp a mechanical advantage of about 2.

Ancient Science in Action

Illustrations carved by the Egyptians in stone suggest that they did indeed use ramps to help build the pyramids. They had neither iron tools nor wheeled vehicles, yet they were able to move huge limestone blocks, some weighing as much as 15 tons. The blocks were chiseled out of solid stone in limestone quarries and then pulled to the pyramids on sleds by a multitude of slaves. The blocks were then hauled up ramps of mud as the pyramid grew higher. When the pyramid was complete, the mud was removed from the top of the pyramid downward, and the pyramid stones were polished.

PROJECT 3

Measure Up

We are used to standard measurements such as feet and inches or meters and centimeters, but it was not always that way. It was the ancient Egyptians who first introduced the idea of a standard unit of measurement. Try this activity to explore some of the standard units the Egyptians used.

Materials

¼-by-1-by-12-inch (.65-by-2.5-by-30-cm) piece of wood
pencil
¼-by-1-by-24-inch (.65-by-2.5-by-60-cm) piece of wood

saw
paper
adult helper

Procedure

1. Place the shorter piece of wood at a right angle to a wall.

2. Place your right foot on the piece of wood with your heel against the wall.

3. Use the pencil to mark the position of the tip of your big toe on the piece of wood.

4. Write "foot" on one side of this piece of wood.

5. Place the longer piece of wood at a right angle to the wall.

6. This time place your elbow against the wall so that your arm and palm are flat on the piece of wood.

7. Use the pencil to mark the position of the tip of your middle finger on the piece of wood.

8. Write "cubit" on one side of this piece of wood.

9. Have your adult helper saw each piece of wood at the mark you made. You now have one measuring stick that is the length of a "foot" and another that is the length of a "cubit."

10. Use each stick to measure several things in your house, such as a table, a door, or the size of the floor in your room. Write down the measurements in "feet" or "cubits."

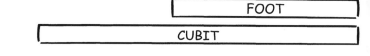

FOOT
CUBIT

More Fun Stuff to Do

For longer measurements, make a "pace" measuring stick. Measure the length of your pace, the distance you travel in one step, on a longer piece of wood. Have an adult helper cut the piece of wood at the mark, then use it to measure the length of several different objects.

Explanation

You should be able to easily measure different objects using either your "foot" or "cubit" measuring stick. In More Fun Stuff to Do, you create a "pace" measuring stick for longer distances.

The ancient Egyptians used the length of the pharaoh's foot as the unit of measurement of a foot and the distance from the pharaoh's elbow to the tip of the middle finger as a unit called the cubit.

One problem with this method of measurement is that it varied from country to country and century to century, depending on who the ruler of the country was. We now have very specific international standards for units of measurements. For example, while a meter was originally 1/1,000,000 of the distance from the Equator to the North Pole of the Earth (39.37 inches), it is now defined as the distance that light travels in 1/299,792,458 seconds.

ANCIENT SCIENCE IN ACTION

Although the ancient Egyptians were the first to use standard measures, it was the Romans who brought some of those measures to the rest of the world. When the ancient Roman armies marched through the ancient world, they were taught to march with a specific rhythm and pace. They also counted the number of paces they went as they traveled from town to town, resting every 1,000 paces. At these 1,000-pace intervals they would put up a stone marker along the side of the road. Over time these markers became a standard unit for measuring longer lengths. The Latin word for 1,000 is "mille," which was later shortened to the word "mile" that we use today. The distance that a Roman soldier would travel in 1,000 paces was approximately 5,280 feet.

PROJECT 4

Keeping Time 1

Quick, what time is it? You can easily answer this question by looking at a wall clock or your watch or even a computer. But how did people tell time before mechanical clocks were invented? The Egyptians invented several ways to use shadows cast by the sun to tell time. The first known sundial was made in the reign of Pharaoh Thutmose III of Egypt in the 15th century B.C.E. Try this activity to make your own sundial and find out how it works.

Materials

8-inch- (20-cm) square piece of thin
    cardboard
10-inch- (25-cm) square piece of thick
    cardboard
pencil

protractor
ruler
scissors
tape
magnetic compass

Procedure

1. Place the square of thin cardboard in the center of the square of thick cardboard. Draw a line around the outside of the thin cardboard, creating an 8-inch (20-cm) square on the inside of the 10-inch (25-cm) cardboard. This is your sundial base.

2. Find the midpoint of two opposite sides of the square you drew by measuring 4 inches (10 cm) from the corners. Connect the midpoints to divide the 8-inch (20-cm) square into equal halves. This line represents 12:00.

3. Using the protractor, measure and mark the angles listed below to the left of the 12:00 line as shown in the diagram. Complete the lines as shown in the diagram and label each line with the corresponding time.

Angle	Time
11°	1:00 P.M.
22°	2:00 P.M.
35°	3:00 P.M.
51°	4:00 P.M.
69°	5:00 P.M.

4. Again using the protractor, measure and mark the angles listed below to the right of the 12:00 line. Complete the lines as shown in the diagram and label each line with the corresponding time.

Angle	Time
11°	11:00 A.M.
22°	10:00 A.M.
35°	9:00 A.M.
51°	8:00 A.M.
69°	7:00 A.M.

5. Use the ruler and pencil to draw a diagonal line on the 8-inch (20-cm) square of thin cardboard.

6. Use the scissors to cut along the line, creating two cardboard triangles.

7. Tape one cardboard triangle along the 12:00 line on the sundial base so that it is perpendicular to the base. Use the protractor to make sure that the triangle is exactly 90 degrees to the base.

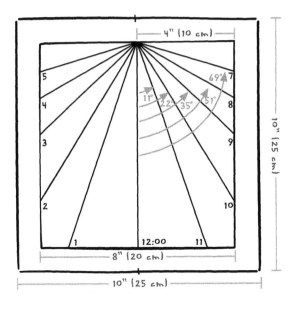

8. Take your sundial outside on a sunny day. Use the compass to align your sundial so that it points north, as shown below. Compare the time on your sundial to the real time. How accurate is it?

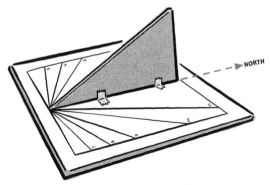

More Fun Stuff to Do

This sundial will be more accurate at latitudes from 40° N to 50° N. If you live outside of those latitudes, how can you correct your sundial? Try methods such as tilting the sundial or changing the angles between hour marks on the sundial face.

Explanation

Your sundial will read a time very close to the time on a watch.

Because the Earth spins on its axis in a counterclockwise motion, it appears that the sun rises in the East and sets in the West. If you place a stick in the ground during the day, it will cast a shadow. That shadow will be longer in the early morning and late evening and will be the shortest at noon. It was the recognition of this fact that led the Egyptians to create the sundial. As the shadow moved across the ground, marks were made to represent an hour. Although each hour in our day is the same length, it has not always been that way. Some early civilizations used hours that had different lengths. Many civilizations decided that there would be a certain number of hours in a day (often 12) and the same number during the night. But since the days are shorter in the winter than in the summer, the daylight hours would be shorter in winter. They would, in fact, vary from day to day, gradually lengthening as summer approached and then becoming shorter again as winter came. If you divide a half-circle into 12 equal parts with the middle mark facing north, then the shadow of the sun on the circle will mark the hour of the day. However, the time that the sun takes to move from line to line will vary with the season and will not be very accurate for use today. To compensate for this, you made your sundial with a different number of degrees between each line. It is very difficult to create a sundial that will be accurate when used in several different locations. A sundial is usually accurate for only one location, and changes have to be made to its design when it is moved.

ANCIENT SCIENCE IN ACTION

The Egyptians also used a shadow clock to tell time in a similar way to a sundial. The shadow clock was made using a pole with a crossbar to cast a shadow on the ground. Marks on the ground were used to tell the time. The shadow clock was easier to make, but was less accurate due to seasonal changes.

The Egyptians were the first to split the time period between sunrise and sunset into 12 equal parts. They also divided the night into 12 equal parts. From this division came the length of time we call the hour and the fact that a day has 24 hours.

Hieroglyphics

The ancient Egyptians may have had the first written language. **Hieroglyphics,** an ancient Egyptian form of writing in which a picture or symbol represents a word, symbol, or sound, have been found that date back to around 3200 B.C.E. The Sumerians developed their own written language, called cuneiform, at about the same time. When ancient Egyptian writing was first discovered, there was no way to translate it because no one had used hieroglyphics for thousands of years. Try this activity to learn more about hieroglyphics.

Materials

pencil
2 sheets of paper
helper

Procedure

1. Write a few simple words, such as "pot" or "cat," on the first sheet of paper.

2. On the second sheet of paper, write out the words in hieroglyphics using the code shown below to change each letter into a symbol.

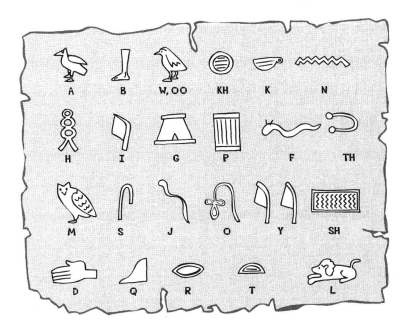

For example, the letter A would be written as . The letter B would be , the letter K (also used for the letter C) would be , and the letter W would be . The word CODE would be written . Notice that there is no symbol for the last E in the word. The Egyptians did not have symbols for most vowel sounds.

3. You can write your words in several ways. Hieroglyphics are written in rows or columns and might be read either from left to right or from right to left. You can figure out which way to read the text by looking at the human and animal figures. These figures always face the beginning of the line. Upper symbols are always read before lower.

4. Give the second sheet of paper to your helper. Ask your helper to use the hieroglyphic code to translate the words by turning each symbol into its corresponding letter.

More Fun Stuff to Do

Hieroglyphics also used a syllabic sign to represent a combinations of letters, as shown below. Try adding them to your hieroglyphic code and writing more words or short sentences.

UR	MEN	NEB
MES	MER	SU
BAT	KHEPER	RA
	SHA	KA

Explanation

Your helper should be able to translate your message using the translation for the symbols.

This activity shows how the ancient Egyptians used a system of symbols to represent letters. In the English language we use an alphabet to represent our spoken words. Most cultures have written languages. Some use alphabets similar to the English alphabet, while others use symbols that are very different. Some cultures, such as the Chinese, use a different symbol for each sound in their language. Other cultures use one symbol for each word or even for a group of words.

ANCIENT SCIENCE IN ACTION

In 1799, near Rosetta, Egypt, French soldiers digging trenches found a stone slab with writing on it. It was written in 197 B.C.E. and inscribed with the same message written in Egyptian hieroglyphics, Egyptian demotic (a popular script used in ancient Egypt), and Greek. Jean François Champollion worked for 14 years to translate the tablet. Because the Greek language was known, he used that as a key and was able to determine what the hieroglyphic symbols meant. The tablet, known as the Rosetta Stone, was the key to deciphering ancient Egyptian hieroglyphic writing.

4 SCIENCE FROM THE CITY-STATES

Ancient Greece

Around 500 B.C.E. an amazing culture began to grow in a group of small **city-states** on the Aegean and Mediterranean Seas. A city-state was an independent city and the surrounding territory directly controlled by it. The brilliance of this culture laid the foundation for the growth of science, politics, sports, and much more in later European civilizations. The ancient Greeks cultivated excellence in a wide range of activities, from sports to music and medicine to mathematics. For over 500 years they influenced everyone with whom they came in contact.

Of particular note were the Greek discoveries in the field of **medicine,** the science of diagnosing, treating, and preventing disease and preserving health. They were the first to study illnesses using a simple form of scientific investigation. The Greeks were very curious about the world around them, and they made many other scientific discoveries, especially in the fields of physics and astronomy.

The Greeks also introduced the concept of democracy. In their government, many people were given a chance to voice their opinions, not just a king. Their free discussion of ideas gave rise to philosophy, reason, logic, and the scientific method. It started an era of great thinkers, men like Aristotle. Aristotle split science into categories, such as biology and physics, and studied them all. The ability to reason and figure things out became important. The Greeks believed that growing intellectually and challenging the mind was a worthwhile end in itself. Many Greek inventions, such as the water wheel and the steam engine, would later be improved by the Romans and the Europeans.

To learn more about some of the things that the Greeks contributed to our world, try the activities in this chapter.

Keeping Time 2

In the previous chapter, you read about the Egyptian sundial, a device that kept time by following the sun's shadow. But what if it was nighttime or just cloudy? Around 330 B.C.E., the Greeks invented a device they called a clepsydra, which measured time by the flow of water. Try the following activity to make your own water clock.

Materials

small nail	tape
2 clear plastic containers (an	water
empty cottage cheese container	several books
and a plastic milk jug work	stopwatch
well)	marking pen

Procedure

1. Use the nail to make a small hole in the bottom of the plastic milk jug. Place a piece of tape over the hole.

2. Fill that container with water and place it on the books. Place the second container on the table below the first container so that the hole in the first container is over the second container.

3. At the same time, start the stopwatch and remove the tape. Water will begin to drip from the top container to the bottom container.

4. After one minute, use the pen to mark the level of the water on the side of the bottom container. Make sure to mark the bottom of the water curve. Continue to mark the water level every minute until all the water is gone.

5. Tape the hole again and refill the top container with the water from the bottom container. Remove the tape. You now have a water clock that tells time. You can estimate the times between the marks.

Explanation

Water will fall from the top milk jug to the lower container. You will be able to read the time from the start of the water falling by looking at the marks on the lower pail.

The water clock works because liquids flow at a constant rate out of a small hole. The Greek clepsydra water clock used water-filled cylinders. When water dripped through the cylinders, a pointer moved and marked the hour on a graduated scale. All timing devices, from the water clock to the digital watch, operate because of the fundamental principal that a regular pattern or cycle operates at a constant rate. In a water clock, the drops of water occur at a known rate. In a grandfather clock, it's the constant swing of a pendulum that is used to tell time. In a modern digital watch, time is measured by the regular vibrations of a quartz molecule.

ANCIENT SCIENCE IN ACTION

Although the water clock was not the best way to tell time, it was centuries before more accurate ways to measure time were invented. In fact, the Italian scientist Galileo used a water clock in the 16th century when he studied the speed at which an object falls to earth due to gravity.

PROJECT 2

The Sound of Music

Many ancient cultures had stringed instruments such as lyres and harps. If you have ever played a modern stringed instrument such as a guitar or violin, you know that you can make music with them by changing the sound a string makes. It was a Greek mathematician named Pythagoras, in the 6th century B.C.E., who first showed mathematically how the length of the strings affected the sound of the music. Try this activity to discover what Pythagoras did.

Materials

hammer

nails

1-by-8-by-24-inch (2.5-by-20-by-
   60-cm) wooden board

1 yard (1 m) of nylon fishing line

metal S hook

plastic pail

rocks

pencils

ruler

adult helper

Procedure

1. Have your adult helper carefully hammer a nail about halfway into the board near one end. Lay the board on a table so that the end opposite the nail is aligned with the edge of the table.

2. Tie one end of the piece of fishing line to the nail. Tie the metal S hook onto the other end of the line.

3. Fill the pail with some rocks and hang it from the S hook. Adjust the length of the fishing line as necessary so that the pail hangs freely.

4. Place two pencils under the line. Pluck the line between the pencils. What happens?

5. Slide the pencils so that they are 8 inches (20 cm) apart under the string. Pluck the string between the pencils. What do you hear?

6. Move the pencils so that they are 4 inches (10 cm) apart. What do you hear this time? Is the sound the same or different than the first sound? Explain.

7. Move the pencils so that they are 12 inches (30 cm) apart. What do you hear this time? Is the sound the same or different from the first sound? Explain.

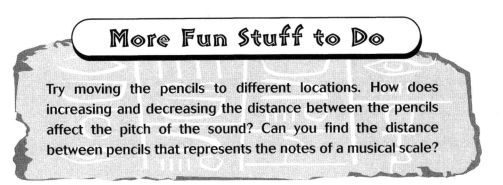

More Fun Stuff to Do

Try moving the pencils to different locations. How does increasing and decreasing the distance between the pencils affect the pitch of the sound? Can you find the distance between pencils that represents the notes of a musical scale?

Explanation

When the length of string between the pencils is changed, the plucked string makes a different sound.

The length of the string between the pencils affects the pitch of the sound made by a stringed instrument. Pitch in music depends on the frequency of the vibration that causes it. The greater the frequency of vibration, the higher the pitch. A shorter length of string gives a higher-pitched sound. Longer lengths give lower-pitched sounds. In general, a string that is half as long as another will vibrate twice as fast as that string and will have a pitch one octave (the eight notes that make a musical scale) higher than the other string. In this activity, the sound the plucked string made when the pencils were 4 inches (10 cm) apart was one octave higher than the one when the pencils were 8 inches (20 cm) apart.

The Greek mathematician Pythagoras (born circa 580 B.C.E.) believed that everything in the world could be ordered and that there were mathematical relationships in many things that we take for granted. He and his students studied music and how the length of a string affected the sound it would make. They discovered that if successive strings were each a fraction of the length of the longest string, they would make the most pleasing sounds to the human ear. Their string lengths became widely used, eventually becoming the eight-note classical musical scale that we still use today. Without this Greek mathematician, music wouldn't sound the same!

PROJECT 3

Eureka!

The Greek scientist Archimedes is said to have discovered a famous scientific principle while taking a bath. He observed that when he lowered his body into a bathtub filled to the top with water, the weight of the water that overflowed the tub was equal to his own weight. Upon realizing this, it is said, he jumped out of the tub shouting "Eureka!" which means "I have found it!" What he had found became known as Archimedes' principle. Try this activity to see how it works.

Materials

cooking pot	string
plastic tub	spring scale (available at most hard-
water	ware or sporting goods stores)
rock	jar (without its lid)

Procedure

1. Place the pot in the plastic tub, then fill the pot with water until it just reaches the top.

2. Tie a string around the rock so you can lift the rock with the string.

3. Hook the spring scale to the end of the string, and use the scale to lift the rock off and weigh it in the air. Record the weight.

4. With the spring scale still attached to the rock, carefully lower the rock into the water-filled pot until it is completely covered. Water should flow from the pot into the plastic tub.

5. Record the weight of the rock now. What happens to the weight of the rock when you weigh it in water?

6. Calculate the difference between how much the rock weighed in the air and how much it weighed in the water by subtracting its weight under water from its weight in the air.

7. Tie another piece of string around the mouth of the jar so you can lift it using only the string.

8. Hook the spring scale to the jar's string and weigh the empty jar.

9. Remove the rock from the pot and the pot from the tub.

10. Pour the water from the tub into the jar.

11. Again hook the spring scale to the jar's string and weigh it filled with water.

12. Calculate the weight of the water by subtracting the weight of the jar by itself from the weight of the jar and water.

13. Compare the weight of the water in the jar to the difference in weight between the rock in the air and the rock in the water. What did you find?

More Fun Stuff to Do

Draw identical horizontal lines halfway up the outside of two Styrofoam cups. Set one cup on the surface of a tub of water. Add marbles to the cup until the water level reaches that mark. Fill the second cup with water until it reaches the same mark. Hold one cup in each hand and compare the weight of the two cups. What do you notice?

Explanation

The weight of the rock when submerged (under water) will be less than its weight in air. When you weigh the water that overflowed the pot when the rock was submerged, you will find that the weight will be the same as the difference between the weight of the rock in air and the weight of the rock in water. In More Fun Stuff to Do, the cup filled with the marbles and the cup filled with water will have the same weight.

This activity demonstrates **Archimedes' principle,** which states that an immersed object is buoyed up by a force equal to the weight of the fluid it displaces. In this activity, the rock weighs less in water than in air. The buoyant force on the submerged rock is equal to the weight of the water displaced.

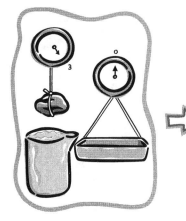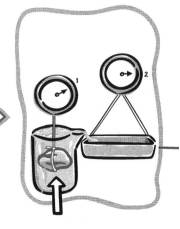

The rock displaces water that has the same weight as the weight loss of the rock due to being in the water.

The buoyant force pushes up with a force of 2. This is equal to the weight of the water the rock displaces.

Archimedes' principle also explains why a boat floats. When an object is in water, buoyancy creates an upward force to counter the force of gravity pulling the object down. When an object like a boat, a surfboard, or even a cup filled with marbles is placed in water, it displaces, or moves, the water. Objects that are placed in water are buoyed up by a force equal to the weight of the water they displace. If the upward buoyancy of the water on a boat is exactly equal to the force of gravity that pulls down on the boat, then the boat floats. To make steel float, the boat must be of a certain shape so as to increase its volume without increasing its weight. This increases the amount of water the boat will displace.

Archimedes' principle is very important in the construction of any boat. Boats must always be built so that the weight of the boat is equal to or less than the weight of the volume of water it will displace.

PROJECT 4

Diving Bell

The Greeks not only investigated what makes objects float on water, they also developed a way for people to explore under water for long periods of time. Try this activity to learn more about what they did.

Materials

string
rock
plastic jar
tape

18-inch (.5-m) or longer piece of
    flexible, plastic aquarium air hose
deep sink or large tub
water

Procedure

1. Use two pieces of string to tie the rock to the mouth of the plastic jar so that the rock hangs about 2 inches (5 cm) directly below the center of the jar's opening. Secure the string in place with tape.

2. Insert one end of the tubing into the jar so it extends into the bottom of the jar. Bend the tubing near the mouth of the jar and tape it to the outside of the jar.

3. Fill the sink or tub with water.

4. Pinch the free end of the tubing closed and place the jar in the water so that the rock hangs below it. The jar should float. If it sinks, use a smaller rock.

5. Release the closed end of the tubing that you previously pinched off. What happens?

6. Blow into the tube. What happens to the jar and rock this time?

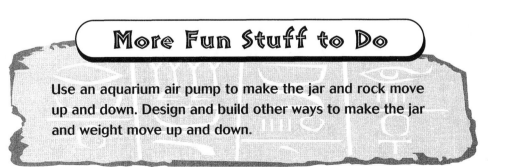

More Fun Stuff to Do

Use an aquarium air pump to make the jar and rock move up and down. Design and build other ways to make the jar and weight move up and down.

Explanation

When you release the closed end of the tubing, the jar and rock sink in the water. When you blow into the tube, the jar and rock rise up in the water and float to the surface.

In this project, you have built a simple diving bell, a bell- or bucket-shaped container that traps air inside when it's put in water upside down. When the jar and rock are first placed in the water and the tube is pinched, the air pressure in the jar is equal to the pressure of the water in the tub, and your diving bell floats. When you release the tube, the water takes the place of the air inside the jar, forcing it out through the tube, and the diving bell is pulled down. By blowing into the tube, you increase the amount and pressure of the air inside the bottle. The air displaces the water in the bottle and the diving bell rises back to the surface of the water. If you use an aquarium pump, as in More Fun Stuff to Do, you achieve the same results, only you use a mechanical device to do the work. This is similar to the way air is pumped to divers in more modern diving bells and diving suits.

Ancient Science in Action

The diving bell was an early invention to help humans extend their time under water. Divers swam into these submerged bells to get air so they didn't have to return to the surface for each breath. Historians say that Alexander the Great used a diving bell with a glass window in about 333 B.C.E. Since then, the diving bell with an air tube running to the surface has been modified into the diving suit.

PROJECT 5

Surprise Attraction

You may have noticed that if you rub your hair with an inflated balloon, your hair will be attracted to the balloon. In 600 B.C.E., the Greek scientist Thales discovered that if he rubbed amber (petrified tree sap) with a piece of wool cloth, small pieces of straw and leather were attracted to the amber. Although Thales did not know why this attraction occurred, he did write that it was an interesting phenomenon. What causes this attraction? Try this activity to find out.

Materials

paper towel

1 teaspoon (5 ml) crispy rice cereal

balloon

wool sweater

Procedure

1. Place the paper towel on the table.

2. Put the cereal on the paper towel.

3. Blow up the balloon and knot the end.

4. Rub the balloon several times on the wool sweater.

5. Bring the balloon near the cereal. Observe what happens.

More Fun Stuff to Do

Try this activity again, but this time try attracting small bits of paper or small pieces of dried grass, each no more than ½ inch (.65 cm) long. Are these small items attracted to the balloon?

Explanation

The cereal is attracted to the balloon, as are small bits of paper and dried grass.

This experiment works because of **static electricity,** which is electricity that does not flow. All objects are made of atoms, and every atom has an equal number of protons and electrons. Protons have a positive charge, and electrons have a negative charge. When these charges are equal, an object is neutral or uncharged. Some objects, however, such as wool or hair, easily lose electrons. When you rubbed the balloon with the wool, some electrons moved from the wool to the balloon. The balloon then had a negative static charge.

When you bring the negatively charged balloon near the crispy cereal, the negatively charged balloon repels the electrons in each piece of cereal. The electrons move to the opposite side of the cereal. This gives the side of the cereal nearest the balloon a positive static charge, and the piece of cereal is attracted to the negatively charged balloon.

After a while, all of the extra electrons will move from the balloon to the cereal. The balloon will become neutral, and the cereal will fall back to the table.

ANCIENT SCIENCE IN ACTION

Although the attraction of objects due to static electricity was discovered by the ancient Greeks, it would take thousands of years before scientists would discover the electrical nature of the atom caused by its electrons, protons, and neutrons. The words *electron, electric,* and *electricity* all come from the Greek word for amber, because later scientists recognized the importance of this first Greek discovery.

PROJECT 6

Knowing All the Angles

The astrolabe was a very sophisticated tool invented by the Greeks that had many uses, including telling time, calculating the positions of celestial objects, and determining latitude. Probably invented around 150 B.C.E., the astrolabe was used for years by many cultures for astronomy and navigation. To learn more about one way to use an astrolabe, try this activity.

Materials

photocopy of the astrolabe drawing in
   this book
scissors
pencil

tape
glue
string
metal washer

Procedure

1. Cut out the copy of the astrolabe drawing from the next page. The drawing can be enlarged if necessary.

2. Fold the top section of the drawing over a pencil and roll it down to the heavy double line to make a tube.

3. Tape the rolled paper tube in place and let the pencil slide out. This is your sighting tube.

4. Glue the bottom section of the astrolabe to a 5-by-8 inch (12.5-by-20 cm) card. Trim the excess card from around the astrolabe.

5. Take an 8-inch (20-cm) piece of string and tie one end to the metal washer.

6. Use the scissors to make a small hole in the middle of the top of the astrolabe below the sighting tube.

7. Thread the free end of the string through the hole and tape it in place.

8. With the string hanging free, sight the top of a tree through the sighting tube.

9. Read the number of degrees by looking where the string touches the astrolabe. What does it read?

10. Try moving farther away from the tree and sighting the top of the tree. What happens to the angle you read on the astrolabe compared to when you were closer?

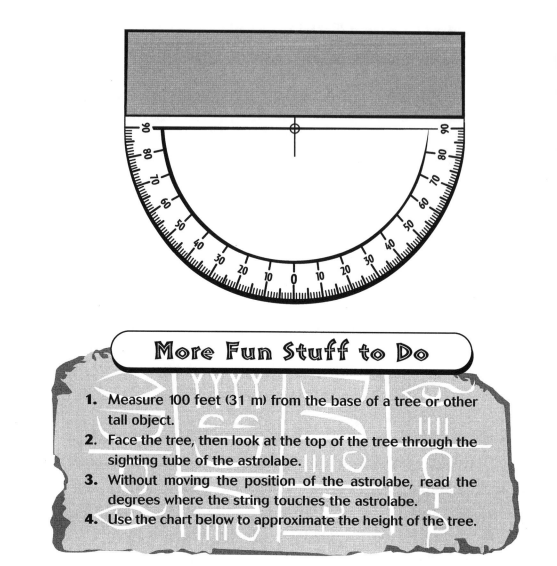

More Fun Stuff to Do

1. Measure 100 feet (31 m) from the base of a tree or other tall object.
2. Face the tree, then look at the top of the tree through the sighting tube of the astrolabe.
3. Without moving the position of the astrolabe, read the degrees where the string touches the astrolabe.
4. Use the chart below to approximate the height of the tree.

Angle (in degrees)	Height of Tree (in ft)	Height of Tree (in meters)	Angle (in degrees)	Height of Tree (in ft)	Height of Tree (in meters)
5	9	2.7	45	102	31.0
10	18	5.4	50	121	36.7
15	27	8.2	55	145	43.9
20	37	11.2	60	176	53.3
25	47	14.4	65	217	65.9
30	59	17.8	70	279	84.5
35	71	21.5	75	379	114.8
40	85	25.8			

Explanation

You used your astrolabe to measure the angle between the tree at eye level and the top of the tree. This angle is measured in degrees. When you move farther away from the tree, as in More Fun Stuff to Do, the angle becomes smaller, so the number of degrees on the astrolabe will become less.

The chart in More Fun Stuff to Do is based on a mathematical principle that the Greeks first noticed called trigonometry. **Trigonometry** is the study of the relationship between the sides and angles of triangles. These relationships are called trigonometric ratios. The ratio you used to find the height of the tree is called the tangent ratio. Trigonometric ratios can find the height of a mountain, the width of a river, or the length of a train without directly measuring them.

The astrolabe made the great Age of Exploration (about 1450–1650) possible by allowing navigators to calculate how far north or south of the equator a ship was.

ANCIENT SCIENCE IN ACTION

One of the earliest astrolabes was designed by a woman, Hypatia of Alexandria, in the 4th century. Astrolabes were borrowed from the Greeks by the Arabs, who improved on their design.

PROJECT 7

Measuring the Earth

You know that the Earth is a sphere because you've seen drawings and possibly even pictures of the Earth from space. But how did ancient people figure out the shape of the Earth? And when they did figure out that the Earth was a sphere, how did they know how big the Earth was? Try this activity to find out how the Greek mathematician Eratosthenes first worked it out.

Materials

tape
2 yards (meters) of string
yardstick (meter stick)
protractor
paper
pencil

calculator
3 helpers—one with you and another
   two who live at least 500 miles
   (800 km) south or north of where
   you live

Note: This activity should be done outside on a sunny day.

Procedure

1. Tape one end of the string to one end of the yard (meter) stick.

2. Go outside at exactly 12:00 noon.

3. Place your yard (meter) stick vertically on a flat area of ground. Use the protractor to ensure that the stick makes a 90° angle with the ground.

4. Turn the yard (meter) stick on its end so that its flat side faces the shadow it casts on the ground.

5. Have your helper place the other end of the string on the tip of the shadow. Shorten the string until it touches the end of the shadow and is taut.

6. Use the protractor to measure the angle the string makes with the yard (meter) stick, and record the data.

7. The helpers who live to the south or north of you should perform the same steps as you.

8. Find out the number of miles (kilometers) away that your helpers live.

9. Get your helpers' data and record it with your own. Subtract the smaller angle from the larger angle in the data.

10. Use the calculator and your data to calculate the radius (the distance from the center to the

edge of a circle or sphere) of the Earth: First divide 360 by the difference of the angles you got in step 9. Then multiply that result by the distance between you and your helpers and divide that answer by 6.28. What answer did you get?

More Fun Stuff to Do

Try this activity with people who live different distances away. How do your answers compare?

Explanation

Your calculation should give you a value of about 3,900 miles (6,400 km).

For example, let's say your helpers lived 550 miles (890 km) south of you. When you each did the experiment, you got an angle of 28 degrees while your helpers got 36 degrees. To use this data for your calculations, you subtract the smaller angle from the larger angle ($36° - 28° = 8°$). Then you divide 360 by this number ($360/8 = 45$). This value is then multiplied by the distance away your helpers are (45×550 miles $= 24,750$ miles or 45×890 km $= 40,050$ km) and divided by 6.28 ($24,750/6.28 = 3,941$ miles or $40,050/6.28 = 6,377$ km). You have calculated the approximate radius of the Earth.

Some ancient cultures imagined the Earth as a flat disk; others even considered it to be a box. The ancient Egyptians said it was egg-shaped. But 2,500 years ago the Greeks decided that the Earth was a sphere. The Greek philosopher Plato argued that since the sphere is a perfect shape, Earth must be spherical. This argument was supported by Aristotle, who observed that Earth cast a round shadow on the moon during a lunar eclipse.

It was a Greek working in Egypt who first measured the radius of the Earth. In 200 B.C.E., the Greek mathematician Eratosthenes was the head of the library in Alexandria. He was told by travelers of a well near the present-day city of Aswan, 500 miles (800 km) south of Alexandria. At noon during the summer solstice, when the sun was directly overhead, the bottom of the well was directly lit by the sun. Using this information, Eratosthenes realized that with a little geometry, he could calculate the radius of Earth by measuring the difference between the angles of the sun's rays at two different locations. His calculations were off by less than 15 percent from the values measured today.

It wouldn't be until 1522, when the Portuguese sailor Ferdinand Magellan and his crew had successfully sailed around the world, that the spherical nature of Earth would be confirmed by direct observation.

ANCIENT SCIENCE IN ACTION

In 1474, an Italian mapmaker using data from the Greek astronomer Ptolemy miscalculated the size of the Earth by many thousands of miles. Because of this mistake, the explorer Christopher Columbus was encouraged to make his historic journey in 1492. He thought that India would be only 2,700 miles (4,320 km) west of the Canary Islands, when the correct calculation would have put it 10,000 miles (16,000 km) away.

PROJECT 8

A Nice Reflection

You probably look in a mirror just about every day and give it little thought. But mirrors can do more than just help you see how you look. They can also tell you something about physics. Mirrors were first used by the ancient Egyptians. Egyptian mirrors were made of polished brass. Other ancient cultures also used mirrors made of different polished metals. But it was a Greek mathematician, Euclid, who first studied the way mirrors reflect. This was the beginning of a field in physics called optics. Try this activity to learn more about mirrors and optics.

Materials

paper	pencil
small piece of modeling clay	large nail
small mirror	ruler

Procedure

1. Place the paper on a table or other flat surface.

2. Use the clay to make a support for the mirror so that it will stand on its own, perpendicular to the table surface.

3. Place the mirror in the clay support so it faces you near the center of the paper. Draw a line on the paper where the front surface of the mirror meets the paper.

4. Balance the nail on its head on the paper so that it stands about 3 inches (7.5 cm) in front of the mirror. Mark the location of the nail on the paper by drawing a small circle around it.

5. Standing near one corner of the paper, close one eye and, with your open eye near the paper, look at the nail's reflection in the mirror. Place the ruler on the paper so that one edge of the ruler is along the imaginary line from your eye to the image of the nail in the mirror. Draw a line on the paper along that edge.

6. Move to the other side of the paper and again look at the nail's reflection in the mirror. Repeat step 5.

7. Remove the mirror from the paper. Place the ruler along the sight lines you drew in steps 5 and 6 and extend them past the line that marked the mirror's surface until they meet on the opposite side of the mirror.

8. Measure the distance from the mirror line to the center of the circle you drew around the nail. Measure the distance from the mirror line to the place where the two sight lines met on the opposite side of the mirror.
What do you notice?

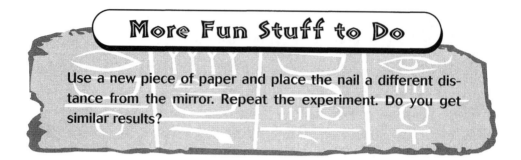

More Fun Stuff to Do

Use a new piece of paper and place the nail a different distance from the mirror. Repeat the experiment. Do you get similar results?

Explanation

The distance from the nail to the mirror should be the same distance as from the mirror to where the two sight lines met.

The field of **optics** studies the properties of light. When light strikes a surface, one thing that happens is reflection. When you looked at the mirror, you saw the reflection of the nail. Light bounced off the nail and traveled in a straight line toward the mirror. This light is called the **incident ray.** Light from the incident ray was then **reflected,** or bounced, off the mirror and traveled in another straight line, called the **reflected ray,** to your eye. The sight lines you drew in this activity showed the paths of the reflected rays. The reflected rays met in a location behind the mirror where the image of the nail is located. In a flat mirror, the image for an object is located the same distance behind the mirror that the object is in front of the mirror.

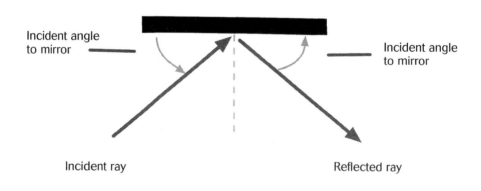

Incident angle to mirror — Incident angle to mirror

Incident ray — Reflected ray

If you were to measure the angle between the incident ray and the mirror and then measure the angle of the reflected ray and the mirror, they would also be equal. This shows a relationship called the **law of reflection.**

The optics of flat mirrors are fairly easy to understand. But if the mirror is either curved in or curved out, different things will happen. Images will be located at a different distance from the mirror and can appear to be either larger or smaller than the object.

About 300 B.C.E., the Greek mathematician Euclid worked out the laws that govern the size and shape of images that mirrors produce, especially mirrors with curved surfaces.

Ancient Science in Action

The ancient Chinese placed mirrors of polished brass on the outside of their doors so that marauding spirits would see themselves and be frightened away. But other ancient mirrors were even scarier. Legend has it that the Greek scientist Archimedes used mirrors as a weapon of war against a Roman fleet that attacked his homeland on the island of Sicily. Archimedes used huge concave mirrors made of polished metal to focus the sun's light on the enemy ships' sails, which reportedly set them on fire.

PROJECT 9

Seeing the Light

A ship traveling at night is trying to find a harbor in which to anchor. In the distance it sees a light that guides it safely through the narrow channel of water at the harbor's mouth and away from the jagged rocks on shore that could sink the ship. The light comes from a lighthouse, an ancient invention that is still used today. The earliest known lighthouse was the Pharos of Alexandria, Egypt, designed by the Greek architect Sostratus in the 3rd century B.C.E. But how does a lighthouse make such a powerful light? Try this activity to find out.

Materials

matches	flat mirror
candle	metal bowl
aluminum pie plate	adult helper

Note: This activity should be done in a dark room, either with curtains covering the windows or at night.

Procedure

1. Have the adult helper use the matches to light the candle and place a few drops of wax on the pie plate. Set the bottom of the candle in the wax until the wax hardens and holds the candle upright.

2. Turn out the lights in the room. Notice how much the candle lights up the room.

3. Hold the flat mirror vertically about 2 inches (5 cm) from the candle flame. What effect does the mirror have on the amount of light in the room?

4. Hold the metal bowl vertically in one hand. Lift the candle and hold it in front of the bowl so that the flame is near the center of the bowl with the bowl opening facing the flame. Try moving the candle slightly closer or slightly further away until you get the maximum amount of light in the room. What effect does the metal bowl have on the amount of light in the room?

5. How much does the candle with the metal bowl light up the room compared to the candle alone? Would the light from the candle, the candle with the mirror, or the candle with the metal bowl be seen from farther away?

Explanation

The candle alone will slightly light the room. When a mirror is used, the half of the room in front of the mirror will become lighter while most of the room behind the mirror will become darker. With the metal bowl, a small area in front of the bowl will become lighter while the rest of the room will become darker.

With no mirrors, the light from the candle will spread out throughout the room. The light is diffused, or spread out evenly, around the room, so it looks about the same from anywhere in the room. If a mirror is added, then the light that strikes the mirror will be reflected and will shine on the other side of the room. This will make the area in front of the mirror lighter than it was with the candle alone, while the area behind the mirror will be darker because very little light reaches it.

When using the metal bowl, you created something called a parabolic reflector. **Parabolic reflectors** have the ability to take light rays that strike them and make them travel out in the same direction. When the light waves from the candle hit the parabolic reflector they bounced off at angles equal to the angles they went in (the Law of Reflection). Because of the way the parabolic reflector is curved, the reflected light waves travel outward in the same direction. So the light from the candle in the metal bowl is brighter than the light from the candle and flat mirror and would be easier to see from a distance.

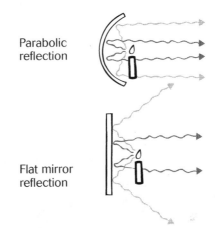

Parabolic reflection

Flat mirror reflection

Parabolic reflectors are used in searchlights, automobile headlights, and lighthouses to make the lights brighter in the direction in which they are pointed.

Ancient Science in Action

One of the Seven Wonders of the Ancient World was the Pharos lighthouse, which stood 350 feet (107 m) high. No one is sure exactly how the lighthouse worked, but some speculate that the light was created by wood and coal burning in a metal basket that was placed in front of a curved, polished metal mirror. It was reported that the light from Pharos was visible from 30 miles (48 km) away! The lighthouse was destroyed, probably by an earthquake, in the mid-14th century.

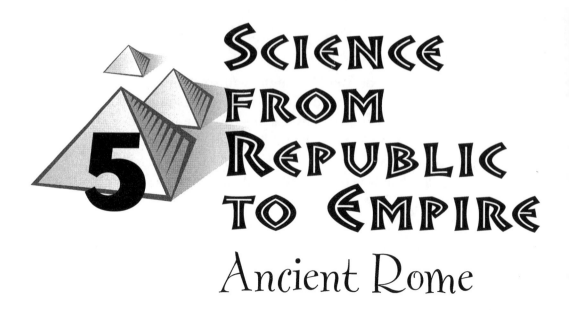

Science from Republic to Empire

Ancient Rome

The Roman Republic began in Italy about 500 B.C.E. and soon became an empire that lasted for almost 1,000 years. At the empire's peak, the Romans controlled the land from England in the north to Egypt in the south, and from Spain in the west to Armenia in the east. The Roman civilization influenced and was influenced by all of the countries it invaded.

Romans introduced and improved several fields in science, such as physics and medicine. They excelled at engineering and built a vast network of roads that linked Rome to the farthest regions of the empire. They built aqueducts to transport water and great meeting places like the Colosseum in Rome, which could hold 50,000 spectators. The Romans also improved upon several Greek inventions, such as the water wheel and simple machines.

To learn more about some Roman inventions and discoveries, try the activities in this chapter.

PROJECT 1

Seeing Better

You probably see many people every day who wear eyeglasses. But have you ever seen an ancient statue of someone wearing glasses? Although there is a statue of the Greek physician Hippocrates using a magnifying glass to examine his patients, it may have been the Romans who first used a shaped lens to improve vision. The Roman writer Seneca was said to have read all the books in Rome by peering at them through a glass globe filled with water. The Roman emperor Nero, in the 1st century C.E., used to hold a lens-shaped jewel in front of his eye in order to better see the gladiatorial games going on in the arena below his royal seating area. Try this activity to learn more about how magnifying lenses and glasses work.

Materials

2-inch- (5-cm) square piece of wax
    paper
newspaper

glass
water
straw

Procedure

1. Place the wax paper over the newspaper. Look at the print on the newspaper. What do you see?

2. Fill the glass with water.

3. Use the straw to transfer a drop of water from the glass to the wax paper.

4. Look at the printing through the water drop. What does it look like this time?

5. Look from the side at the drop of water. What does it look like?

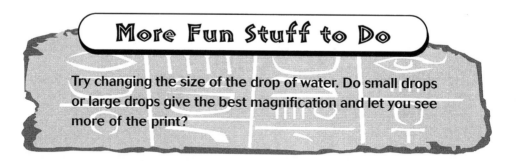

More Fun Stuff to Do

Try changing the size of the drop of water. Do small drops or large drops give the best magnification and let you see more of the print?

Explanation

When you first look at the print through the wax paper, the letters are the same size as on the printed page. However, when you look at the same letters through the drop of water, the letters look bigger. The drop acts as a lens to magnify the letters underneath. When you look at the drop from the side, you can see that it is curved on the top.

Depending on how a lens is curved, objects viewed through the lens can appear larger or smaller. A **lens** is a piece of glass or other transparent substance with a curved surface that **refracts** or bends and brings together rays of light passing through it. Light rays from the object you are looking at pass through the lens. Because the lens is curved, light rays going through the top and bottom of the lens are bent more than light rays going through the middle of the lens. The light rays all meet at what is called the "focus of the lens."

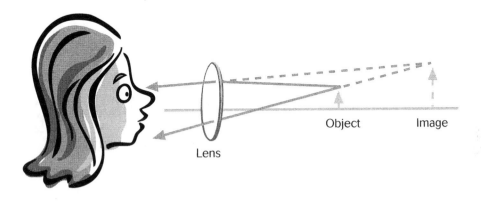

Lens   Object   Image

A lens can be used in many ways, such as in telescopes, microscopes, eyeglasses, and contact lenses.

Ancient Science in Action

Around 1000 C.E., the "reading stone" (what we know as a magnifying glass) was developed. A segment of a glass sphere was laid on reading materials to magnify the letters. Although the exact origin of spectacles (glasses worn by humans to improve their vision) isn't known, it is known that people wore quartz-lens glasses by the end of the 13th century. The first bifocals were made in America in 1775 by Benjamin Franklin. (Bifocals are spectacles in which one part of the lens is curved for seeing things up close and another part is curved for seeing things that are far away.)

PROJECT 2

Clever Clippers

The oldest scissors were made in 1500 B.C.E. They consisted of two bronze blades joined by a spring. In about 100 C.E., the Romans greatly improved on the design of scissors by joining two blades of iron or bronze at a pivot point. This lever design increased the force in the cutting action and made the scissors easier to use. Try this activity to learn more about how the lever action of scissors helps them work better.

Materials

paper   scissors
sharp knife   adult helper

Procedure

1. Have your adult helper hold a sheet of paper vertically with one hand by the top of the paper and try to cut it in half using the knife. How well does the knife work for cutting paper?

2. While your helper is doing this, take another piece of paper and use the scissors to cut the piece of paper in half. How well do the scissors work for cutting paper?

Explanation

It will be easier to cut the paper using scissors than with a knife.

A lever is an example of a simple machine. A **lever** is made of a rigid board or bar that is supported at a fixed point called a fulcrum. Levers make it easier to lift heavy loads because they magnify the force exerted; in other words, they turn a small force into a big one. You can use a lever to lift a heavy load by setting the load someplace on the lever and positioning the fulcrum in the proper location. The exact force needed to lift the load will depend on the length of the lever and the location of the fulcrum.

The scissors are a form of lever as well. Your fingers exert a force on the end of the scissors where the handles are. The fulcrum is the pivot point of the scissors. In this case, the lever does not lift an object, but the force that is created is used to push the blades together to cut paper.

Ancient Science in Action

Ancient records show that levers were used as early as 3000 B.C.E. The shadoof, a counterweighted lever system, was used by the Egyptians to lift water from rivers. A counterweight is a weight used to balance one end of a lever. The shadoof was made of a pole with a rock attached to one end as the counterweight and a rope and bucket attached to the other end. The bucket was lowered into the river and filled with water. The rock on the other end of the shadoof made lifting the water-filled bucket easier. The shadoof is still used in some countries.

PROJECT 3

Powerful Wheels

The water wheel was very important to the ancient Romans. Although water wheels had been used by the Greeks, they saw the water wheel more as a novelty to be observed than as a device to do work. The water wheel was improved upon by the Romans, who connected their water wheel axles to wheeled gears to transmit its turning motion to other wheels. These turning wheels could then turn a millstone, a large wheel made of solid stone that rolled on another stone, to grind grains into flour. Try this project to learn how water energy can be used to do work.

Materials

8 small plastic spoons
Styrofoam ball
pliers or wire cutters
coat hanger
file
glue

two 1-inch (2.5-cm) pieces of
    plastic drinking straw
string
bolt
adult helper

1. Push the handle end of each spoon into the Styrofoam ball. The spoons should be placed an equal distance apart around an imaginary equator line for the ball. The bowl of each spoon should face the back of the spoon in front of it.

2. Have your adult helper use the pliers or wire cutters to cut an 18-inch (45-cm) piece of wire from the coat hanger and file down any rough edges. This will be the axle.

3. Insert the wire through the north pole of the ball and push until it exits at the south pole. This gives you a water wheel. Glue the wire to the ball at the pole ends of the ball.

4. Slide one piece of plastic straw onto each end of the coat hanger wire. To test your water wheel, hold the straws and blow on the spoons or popsicle sticks. The spoons should catch the wind and turn the water wheel.

5. Hold your water wheel by grasping one straw piece with each hand. Place the water wheel under a tap so that the bowls of the spoon are directly under the flowing water. What happens?

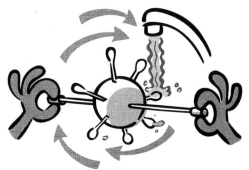

6. Tie one end of a 12-inch (30-cm) piece of string to a bolt. Tie the other end of the string to the wire between the Styrofoam ball and one piece of plastic straw.

7. Again hold your water wheel under a tap so that the string and bolt hang down and the bowls of the spoon are directly under the flowing water. What happens this time?

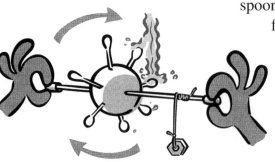

Try to come up with other ways to make your water wheel do work. For example, place a wheel on one end of the wire to simulate a mill stone (a large round rock used to grind grains). How could the rotating stone be used to make flour?

Explanation

When the water strikes the plastic spoons, it will cause the Styrofoam ball to turn. The turning ball will turn the wire, and the string will wind onto the wire. As the string winds onto the wire, the bolt will be lifted.

This is an example of an energy transformation. In an energy transformation, one form of energy is changed into another form. In this activity, the energy in the falling water causes the ball to spin. The spinning ball causes the wire to turn and the string to wind onto the wire. This transforms the energy again, using it to do work, to lift the bolt.

This activity shows the actions involved in ancient water-wheel-driven mills. Water-wheel mills are usually built on large rivers. A dam is constructed to stop the flow of water and form a large storage lake behind it called a **reservoir.** When energy is needed to drive a water wheel, water from the reservoir is allowed to flow through a

ANCIENT SCIENCE IN ACTION

By 1086, there were over 5,000 water-wheel-driven mills operating in England. Later, the power in falling water was used in other ways. In 1880, the first hydroelectric power plant in North America was built in Niagara Falls, New York. Today much of the electrical energy that we use comes from **hydroelectricity,** electrical energy generated from the gravitational energy of falling water. In a hydroelectric plant, there is a special kind of water wheel called a **turbine.** The turbine drives a generator that produces electricity.

tube. The rushing water from the tube spins a water wheel. In an ancient water-wheel-driven mill, the water wheel was connected to a large millstone that would turn on another stone. Grains are placed between the stones, and the rolling action grinds the grains into flour.

Stronger Structures

The first bridges that humans used to cross rivers were probably fallen logs. A log or beam supported on either end by land or by piers is called a beam bridge. But the Romans developed a kind of bridge that is stronger and can span greater distances than the beam: the arch bridge. Try this activity to find out how much more an arch bridge can support than a beam bridge.

Materials

2 strips of thin cardboard, each
  6 by 18 inches (15 by 45 cm)
scissors

several books
ruler
plastic figures

Procedure

1. Cut one of the cardboard strips so that it is 12 inches (30 cm) long.

2. Make two piles of books so that each is 6 inches (15 cm) high and the piles are 8 inches (20 cm) apart.

3. Place the shorter piece of cardboard across the top of the books, creating a bridge between the two piles of books.

4. Place a plastic figure in the middle of the cardboard span. Does your bridge support the weight of one plastic figure?

5. Continue to add plastic figures to the middle of the cardboard span. How many plastic figures can it hold?

6. Bend the longer strip of cardboard and place it between the two piles of books so that it makes an arch. The ends should touch the bases of the piles of books, and the peak should be at the

same height as the piles of books. You may need to move the piles slightly closer or farther apart to have the arch at the right height.

7. Lay the shorter strip of cardboard across the top of the books and the arch.

8. Again place a plastic figure in the middle of the cardboard span. Does your bridge support the weight of one plastic figure? Continue to add plastic figures to the middle of the cardboard span. How many plastic figures can this structure hold?

Beam bridge

Arch bridge

More Fun Stuff to Do

Try making arches out of pieces of cardboard that are different widths or thicknesses. Can you make a structure that holds the most weight?

Explanation

The cardboard across the span will hold only a few plastic figures before collapsing under the weight. With the arch below the span, the structure will be able to hold more weight.

The first important architectural invention to span an open space was the post-and-beam construction, in which two upright posts support a horizontal beam. (This is similar to a beam bridge, where the beam is supported by land on either end.) Stone and wooden beams are strong when under compression (squeezed) but weak under tension, when they are stretched. When a stone or log is used as a beam it is under tension and can break rather easily.

The ancient Romans used the arch structure to solve this problem. When weight is placed on top of the arch, the stones that make up the arch are compressed, rather than placed under tension, making the stone structure much stronger.

ANCIENT SCIENCE IN ACTION

The most amazing arch structures built by the ancient Romans were aqueducts. These aqueducts carried water through valleys and rivers to the many cities throughout the Roman Empire. The water ran in canals at the top of several rows of arches. The longest Roman aqueduct was the Aqueduct of Carthage in Tunisia in Northern Africa. It was 88 miles (141 km) long and could carry 7 million gallons (31.8 million L) of water a day, enough to fill 200,000 bathtubs. Several of the arches needed to support the aqueduct's weight as it traveled across valleys are still standing.

PROJECT 5

Stronger Materials

As you saw in the previous activity, the Romans built aqueducts to carry water from its source in the mountains to where it was needed in other parts of their empire. But water is very heavy, and the structures they built needed to be strong to support the weight of the water. The arch design made for a stronger structure, but the Romans also developed stronger building materials. First they perfected concrete, using a mixture of lime, ash from a particular volcano, chunks of rock and/or sand, and water. Concrete was very strong, but the Romans then found a way to make it even stronger. Try this activity to see how.

Materials

felt pen

clean, dry kitchen sponge

several books

small jar

marbles

3 bamboo skewers

Procedure

1. Use the felt pen to draw lines about ¼ inch (.6 cm) apart along the edges of the long side of the sponge.

2. Place the sponge so its ends rest on two piles of books. Place a small jar on the center of the sponge. Add a few marbles to the jar to test the strength of the sponge bridge. What happens? What do the lines on the sponge do?

3. Push two bamboo skewers through the length of the sponge and again place the sponge on the piles of books.

4. Place the jar on the center of the sponge and add marbles to test the strength of the bridge. What happens this time?

Explanation

When the marbles are put in the jar on the sponge, the sponge will bend. The lines near the top of the sponge will become slightly shorter (undergo compression), while the lines near the bottom of the sponge will become longer (undergo tension). When the bamboo skewers are put through the sponge, the sponge will not bend as much, so the lines will not change.

This activity shows a way to make a stronger building material called reinforced concrete. A structure that bears weight has to be designed so that the forces created by the load on the structure (the weight of the structure and other forces such as the wind that act on it) are directed through the structure and into the ground. There are two basic ways in which forces can be moved through structures: pulling and pushing. The materials of a structure are either stretched by the load and undergo tension, or are pushed by the load and undergo compression. For example, when you pull on a rubber band, it becomes longer and undergoes tension. When you squeeze a sponge, it becomes smaller and undergoes compression. Since building materials are much stronger than rubber bands or sponges, their lengthening under tension and shortening under compression are not as obvious to the naked eye, but they always occur.

Since all structural actions consist of tension and/or compression, all structural materials must be strong in one or both. Different materials have different abilities to withstand tension or compression. Concrete is strong under compression. Bronze and other metals are strong under tension. If you combine the compressive strength of concrete with the tensile strength of bronze (or nowadays steel), you have a very strong form of reinforced concrete, which is good for many practical uses.

Cement is actually an ingredient in concrete, although many people use the words concrete, cement, and mortar to mean the same thing. Cement is usually made by mixing powdered limestone with powdered clay and heating it in a kiln (oven) to produce a fine gray powder. **Concrete** is made by mixing cement with sand and water. The concrete can be made stronger by adding rock pieces, called aggregate. When concrete hardens, it feels like a stone and is very strong. Mortar is made by mixing cement with sand, lime, and water. It isn't as strong as a concrete, but the lime gives the mixture a stickiness that makes it good for holding other pieces of stone together.

ANCIENT SCIENCE IN ACTION

The first example of reinforced concrete was found in a beam over the door of an ancient Roman tomb built over 2,000 years ago. The beam was reinforced with bronze rods. This same building technique was later found in other ancient Roman structures such as aqueducts. Modern steel-reinforced concrete was invented in France in the 1850s.

SCIENCE FROM THE FAR EAST

Ancient China

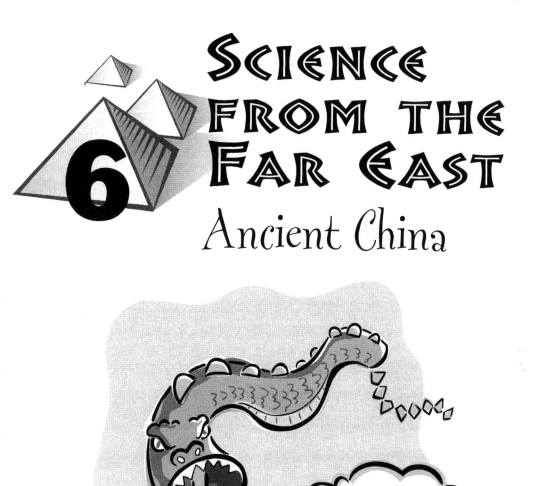

The Chinese civilization developed largely in isolation from the rest of the world because it was physically separated by mountains, deserts, and oceans. The earliest Chinese people settled in the fertile lands around the Yellow River over 12,000 years ago. By 4700 B.C.E., they were cultivating rice and other grains, and by 1500 B.C.E. they had mastered the technology of bronze making. Over the next thousand years they would master new technologies such as iron working and firing pottery in high-temperature kilns.

The ancient Chinese studied astronomy, the science that investigates the motion and composition of the stars and planets, and **chemistry,** the science that investigates matter. The Chinese also introduced several important discoveries, including paper and gunpowder, to the rest of the world. When the Italian explorer Marco Polo traveled east and visited Beijing, the capital of China, in the 13th century, he found a magnificent city with wonders he had never seen before in the West.

To learn more about some Chinese discoveries, try the activities in this chapter.

PROJECT 7

Flying High

People have long been fascinated by flight and have tried many ways to overcome Earth's gravity. Kites marked our first success in soaring into the air. Kites were first flown by the Chinese as early as 1080 B.C.E. In this activity, build a special kite called a sled kite and experience the fascination firsthand.

Materials

plastic garbage bag, at least 24 by 30 inches (60 by 75 cm)
scissors
yard (meter) stick
marking pen

duct tape or packing tape
two wooden dowels, 24 inches (60 cm) long and ⅛ inch (3 mm) in diameter
string

Procedure

1. Flatten the plastic garbage bag on a large tabletop and cut out a rectangular piece that is 24 by 30 inches (60 by 75 cm). Lay the rectangular piece of plastic flat on the table in front of you with the long sides on top and bottom.

2. On the bottom edge, measure in 6 inches (15 cm) from each end and mark the plastic with a marking pen. Measure in 6 inches (15 cm) from each end of the top edge and mark the plastic.

3. Along each side edge, measure down 8 inches (20 cm) from the top and mark the plastic. Use the yard (meter) stick to draw lines between the 6-inch (15-cm) and 8-inch (20-cm) marks on each side as shown.

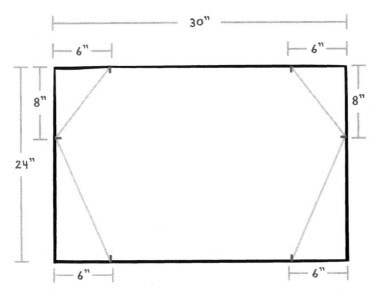

4. Cut out the six-sided piece of plastic.

5. Place a small piece of duct tape sticky side up on the top and bottom edges at each spot where you drew a 6-inch (15-cm) mark. Place the tape so that half of it is stuck to the plastic and the other half is free.

6. Place the wooden sticks vertically between the pieces of tape on each side. Fold the tape over to secure the sticks to the plastic.

7. Place two more small pieces of duct tape sticky side up on the 8-inch (20-cm) marks on each side of the kite. Again place the tape so that half of it is stuck to the plastic and the other half is free.

8. Cut a piece of string 2 yards (2.2 meters) long. Place the ends of the string on the exposed tape with enough string left over on the ends so that you can later tie knots. Fold the tape over the string and secure it to the plastic. Tie the string in a knot around the tape.

9. Lift the kite by the string and determine the center of the string. If you fold the kite exactly in half, this should be easy. Tie a knot in the center of the string.

10. Tie the end of the remaining string to the knot. Your kite is ready to fly!

More Fun Stuff to Do

Try making your kite out of newspaper or other material. How does it work? Can you design a kite that will fly better?

Explanation

In this activity, you made a kite that will fly even with only light wind.

No one knows exactly who first invented the kite. According to one story, kite makers in the 4th century B.C.E. made kites shaped like birds. It was said that these kites, which were designed to mimic the flight of birds and butterflies, could fly for up to three days. Later kites took the shapes of dragons and other flying things. According to another story, a Chinese general, Huan Theng, had the idea for a kite after noting the way his hat flew from his head in the wind. He then thought of a way that kites could be used in battle. He would attach bamboo whistles onto the strings of many kites and have them flown above the heads of the enemy. The whistles would shriek so loudly in the wind that the enemy would believe they were plagued by evil spirits and run away.

Kites fly because of air flow. The Chinese didn't know exactly why kites would fly. It was a scientist named Daniel Bernoulli in the 1700s who figured that out. **Bernoulli's principle** says that when air flows, its pressure decreases when its speed increases. Because of the way a kite is shaped, the wind blowing over the top of the kite speeds up, which results in a decrease in air pressure above the kite. The kite is then lifted into the air by the higher pressure from below.

The kite you made is called a sled kite. This kite has a special design that makes it very stable in flight. The two wooden sticks along both sides and the long bridle (the string that attaches one side of the kite to the other) create a large area of the kite that is exposed to the wind. This design allows the kite to remain in an upright position and to fly in very light wind.

ANCIENT SCIENCE IN ACTION

Kites were brought to Europe by the Dutch around 1600. In the early 1800s, kite power was used by a British schoolteacher to pull a lightweight carriage holding four people at 20 mph (32 km/h). Kites were also used in manned flight experiments. Of particular note is the box kite, invented in 1893 by the Australian Lawrence Hargrave. Its shape inspired the aircraft design used by the Wright brothers and other aviation pioneers.

PROJECT 2

Going Up with a Bang!

Chinese chemists accidentally discovered gunpowder in the 8th century while experimenting to find medicines that would prolong life. During the 9th century, the Chinese were using the gunpowder to make fireworks for use as military signals and in celebrations such as New Year's. We don't want you to experiment with real gunpowder, but you can still get a bang out of this activity and learn more about chemical reactions.

Materials

safety glasses
newspaper
empty plastic film canister with lid

water
Alka-Seltzer tablet

Procedure

1. Put on the safety glasses. Cover your table or work area with newspaper.

2. Fill a plastic film canister half full of water.

3. Break the tablet of Alka-Seltzer into quarters. Place one quarter of the tablet in the water. Do not put the top on the container. Watch what happens when the tablet touches the water.

4. Empty the canister and refill it with fresh water.

5. Take another quarter tablet of Alka-Seltzer and place the tablet in the water. Quickly and firmly put the top on the canister. Set the "loaded" canister upright at least 3 feet (1 meter) away from you. What happens?

More Fun Stuff to Do

Experiment to see if you can make the canister lid fly higher. Try using different amounts of water or Alka-Seltzer tablets.

Explanation

When you first add the Alka-Seltzer tablet to the water in the canister, it will bubble. When you add the Alka-Seltzer tablet to the water in the canister and replace the lid, after a few moments the lid will fly up into the air.

This is an example of a **chemical reaction** that produces explosive results. In a chemical reaction, a change in matter takes place in which substances break apart to produce one or more new substances. The Alka-Seltzer tablet contains a substance called bicarbonate. When you mix bicarbonate with water a new substance, carbon dioxide gas, is formed. When you put the top on the container, the carbon dioxide gas is trapped. The pressure of the gas builds up until it is strong enough to pop the top off the container.

Chinese fireworks used gunpowder for their chemical reaction. Gunpowder is a blackish mixture of sulfur, charcoal dust, and saltpeter. Modern fireworks use different chemicals, and there are actually two chemical reactions that take place. The first chemical reaction happens at the bottom of a tube that causes a fireworks ball to fly up into the air (in a process similar to the flying canister lid). Once the ball is in the air, a second chemical reaction occurs that causes the ball to explode. The different shapes and colors of the exploding fireworks are caused by different shapes of the fireworks ball and by the addition of other chemicals to the exploding mixture.

ANCIENT SCIENCE IN ACTION

By the 10th century, the Chinese had further improved gunpowder's explosive power and had invented the gun, the rocket, the bomb, and the mine. The Chinese army was the first to use both guns and rockets in battle, against the invading Mongols in the early 13th century at the battle of Kai-Keng. Following the battle, the Mongols began to make gunpowder and rockets of their own and eventually conquered China. It is thought that the Mongols were responsible for the spread of gunpowder to Europe.

PROJECT 3

Write On

Ancient humans wrote on many different substances, such as papyrus (reeds from Egypt), parchment (inside lining on sheep or lambskin) and even bark (Native North Americans). But it was the Chinese in about 100 B.C.E. who first made the kind of paper we know. What is paper, and how is it made? Try this activity to find out.

scrap paper
bucket
warm water
blender
plastic tub, about 6 by 12 by 18
  inches (15 by 30 by 45 cm)
2 old towels

sponge
9-by-9-inch (22.5-by-22.5-cm)
  piece of cardboard
scissors
8-by-8 inch (20 by 20 cm)
  square piece of screen
duct tape

Note: Be sure to ask for adult permission before you use the blender.

Procedure

1. Tear the paper into small squares about 1 inch (2.5 cm) on a side. You'll need about 5 large handfuls.

2. Place the paper in the bucket and add warm water until the paper is just covered. Let the paper soak for an hour, pour off the old water, then again add warm water to cover the paper. Let the paper soak for another hour or until it is very soggy and wet.

3. Fill the blender half full of water. Add a handful of soggy paper from the bucket, then turn the blender on to its lowest setting and let it run for a couple of minutes.

4. Fill the plastic tub half full of water. Add the blender mixture to the tub.

5. Repeat steps 3 and 4 until all the soaked paper has been blended.

6. Wet one old towel and place it on the table next to the plastic tub of blended paper.

7. Cut a 7-by-7-inch (17.5-by-17.5-cm) square hole in the center of the cardboard. Place the screen so it overlaps all sides of the cardboard and fasten it in place with duct tape.

8. Stir the blended paper in the tub until it is well mixed.

9. Hold the screen square by opposite sides and slide it into the mixture. Pull the screen straight up, making a layer of blended paper on the top of the screen.

10. Hold the screen over the tub until the water stops dripping.

11. Turn the screen upside down on the towel. Remove the screen from the paper layer by lifting one edge, then peeling off the screen.

12. Place a dry towel on the paper layer and gently press on it to remove more water.

13. Set the paper layer aside to dry overnight.

14. Keep making paper until all the blender paper is gone.

Note: Do not pour the blender paper down the drain! Strain it through a piece of cloth to remove the water, then throw the remainder into the trash.

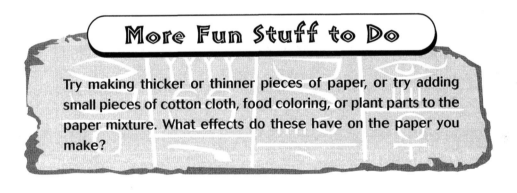

More Fun Stuff to Do

Try making thicker or thinner pieces of paper, or try adding small pieces of cotton cloth, food coloring, or plant parts to the paper mixture. What effects do these have on the paper you make?

Explanation

You made a thick piece of paper from a mixture of old paper and water. In More Fun Stuff to Do, you made paper that has different textures and colors.

In this activity, you made paper in much the same way that the ancient Chinese did, except that instead of recycling old paper, they used the bark of trees and scraps of cloth. A modern paper manufacturing company makes paper mostly from trees. Trees, like all living things, are made of cells. Their cells are surrounded by a special material that makes a **cell wall.** The cell walls in a tree are made of long, thin fibers, which are special because they can absorb water.

This causes the fibers to stick together. Similar fibers are also found in cotton, which can also be used in making paper.

When you put the paper in the blender, you are not only chopping the paper into small pieces but also forcing the water and fibers together. When you lift the screen, you create a layer of paper. As the water drains away, the fibers are forced closer and held together by their rough edges. The longer the fibers, the stronger the paper they will make.

ANCIENT SCIENCE IN ACTION

In 105 C.E. the Chinese court official Tsai Lun toured China to survey the techniques that were being used to make paper. In reporting the results of his trip to the emperor, he related that the best paper was made from a soupy mixture of the bark of trees combined with scraps of cloth, old fishing nets, and rope fibers. News of Tsai Lun's report spread quickly throughout China, and the practice of making paper began. Tsai Lun is still called the "father of paper."

In 751, during a battle in central Asia between Arab and Chinese armies, the Arabs captured two Chinese paper makers, who gave them the secret of paper making. By the 12th century, Arab merchants had opened the first European paper mill in Spain.

PROJECT 4

Cool Treats

We aren't the only ones who like cool treats in the summer. Both Alexander the Great in about 400 B.C.E. and the Roman emperor Nero around 4 B.C.E. sent slaves to the mountains for snow and ice so that they could have what we would now call "ices," shaved ice and snow mixed with puréed fruit and juice, then sweetened with honey. During China's Tang Dynasty (618–907 C.E.), something similar to ice cream was made from the frozen milk of cows, goats, and buffalo, flavored with camphor and thickened with flour. Sounds disgusting, but at least it was a start. Try this activity to make some of your own ice cream.

Materials

¹⁄2 cup (125 ml) milk
1 teaspoon (5 ml) sugar
¹⁄2 teaspoon (2.5 ml) vanilla
small resealable freezer bag
large resealable freezer bag

ice
1 teaspoon salt
towel
spoons
helper

Procedure

1. Pour the milk, sugar, and vanilla into the small bag. Seal the bag, squeezing out all the air.

2. Fill the large bag half full of ice. Add the salt to the ice.

3. Place the small bag into the larger bag filled with ice.

4. Seal the larger bag, again squeezing out the air.

5. Wrap the larger bag in a towel. Take turns with your helper moving, shaking, and rolling the towel with the bag for about 20 minutes.

6. Open the larger bag and remove the smaller bag. What has happened to the milk? Try a taste of the mixture. How is it?

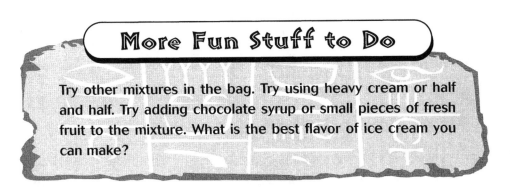

More Fun Stuff to Do

Try other mixtures in the bag. Try using heavy cream or half and half. Try adding chocolate syrup or small pieces of fresh fruit to the mixture. What is the best flavor of ice cream you can make?

Explanation

After about 20 minutes, the mixture will begin to freeze and you will have a simple form of ice cream.

The flavor of ice cream comes from the milk, sugar, and vanilla or other flavorings that you add. The frozen texture comes from the mixture of ice and salt in the outside bag. The freezing point of pure water is 0° C. This temperature would not be low enough to freeze the milk and turn the mixture into ice cream. But by adding salt to the ice, you lower its freezing point. The temperature of the ice can be lowered to between –5° and –10° C, depending on the amount of salt that is added. This temperature is low enough for the milk to freeze and ice cream to form.

ANCIENT SCIENCE IN ACTION

According to legend, the Venetian explorer Marco Polo brought the recipe for ice cream home from China after his first visit there in the 13th century. It may be a myth, but we do know that the first ice cream in Italy was made around that time, and its popularity quickly spread. Ice cream was brought by the Italian Catherine de Medici to the French court on her marriage to the future Henry II in 1533. Supposedly her Italian chefs served 34 different flavors of ice cream, one on each day of her wedding celebration. From there the recipe for ice cream continued to spread throughout Europe and later to the United States. George Washington, the first president of the United States, spent $200 on ice cream in just two months. However, history does not tell us his favorite flavor!

PROJECT 5

True North

The first mention of the magnetic compass appeared in Chinese writing around 1060. The Chinese discovered that an iron needle magnetized by rubbing it with lodestone (a naturally magnetic form of an iron mineral) that was stuck in a piece of straw and floated in a bowl of water would always point north. The magnetized needle of the compass always aligns with Earth's North and South Poles because the Earth acts as a natural magnet. Here's how you can make a magnetic compass similar to the ones the Chinese designed.

Materials

Styrofoam plate   strong magnet
scissors   bowl
sewing needle   water

Note: Be very careful when handling the sewing needle; it is very sharp.

Procedure

1. Cut a 1-inch (2-cm) diameter disk from a Styrofoam plate.

2. Magnetize a sewing needle by rubbing it against a strong magnet 30 or 40 times. Always rub the needle in the same direction. You can tell if the needle is magnetized when it attracts another needle to it, just like a real magnet.

3. Insert the needle lengthwise through the Styrofoam disk.

4. Place the disk in a bowl of water. What happens?

More Fun Stuff to Do

Use a real compass to determine north, south, east, and west. In what direction does the needle in the bowl point? Write N, S, E, and W on pieces of tape and stick the tape in the right locations on the bowl. The needle aligns itself with the Earth's magnetic field until it finally stops when pointing north.

Explanation

The needle will point at the north magnetic pole of the Earth.

Magnetism is the form of energy that causes some substances to attract or repel other substances. All magnetism is caused by moving electrons. In permanent magnets, the spin of electrons in orbit around the nucleus of the atom creates the magnetic effect. Although all matter has electrons in orbit around their nucleus, in magnetic objects the atoms are all lined up so that they point in the same direction. By rubbing a nonmagnetic needle against a magnet, you cause the atoms in the needle to line up in the same direction, and the needle becomes magnetic.

The Earth has a large magnetic field due to the movement of the molten magma in the Earth's core. This magnetic field can be detected on the Earth's surface with other magnets. The needle of a compass lines up automatically with the Earth's magnetic field.

ANCIENT SCIENCE IN ACTION

The fact that a magnet would align with the Earth's magnetic field was discovered by accident almost 2,000 years ago. Legend has it that the Chinese magician Luan Te played a game similar to chess in which one of the game pieces was a round-bottomed spoon. When he emptied the metal playing pieces onto the board, the spoon landed on its rounded bottom and began to spin around. When it stopped spinning, the handle of the spoon was pointed north. It turned out that the spoon was made from lodestone and would align itself with the Earth's magnetic field. The Chinese first used such devices not as direction pointers, but for geomancy, the technique of aligning buildings according to the forces of nature.

But the Chinese continued to refine their magnetic compasses. First came the turtle compass, a wooden turtle with a piece of lodestone in its belly and an iron needle pushed through its tail to balance the lodestone. When the turtle was balanced on a sharp piece of bamboo, the needle would point north. The first liquid compass used a piece of magnetized iron in the shape of a fish that was floated in a bowl of water. The Chinese began experimenting with other metals and discovered that a mixture of iron and carbon would produce steel, a metal that is stronger than iron and holds its magnetism for a very long time. Further refinements occurred with the development of the box compass, which was used for navigation on ships. By the early 1200s, Chinese ships were sailing far from shore aided by their magnetic compasses.

PROJECT 6

Count on It

When you have a math problem to do, you probably use a calculator. But before there were calculators, there were other devices to aid in counting. The oldest surviving counting board is the Salamis tablet, used by the Babylonians around 300 B.C.E. There are also examples of Greek and Roman counting boards. The counting board was used to keep track of the number of items being counted and was a big help when trade began between communities. But it is the Chinese who are credited with the invention of one of the best counting devices: the bead-frame counting board, commonly called the abacus. Try this activity to learn how the abacus works.

Materials

25 pennies
10 nickels

Procedure

1. Lay the pennies flat on the table.

2. Make five columns of pennies, each with five pennies. The columns should have a small distance between them.

3. Above each column of pennies, make a shorter column of two nickels. The nickel column should be about 2 inches (5 cm) above the top row of pennies.

4. Here's how to count using your counting table. Always begin with the right column of pennies. To count 1, you move the top penny up one space. To count 2, you move the next penny up and so on to the count of 5.

5. Once you reach 5, you push the bottom nickel down a space and push the 5 pennies down into their original places.

6. To count 6, push the top penny in the same column up again. It counts six because you add the penny value, 1, to the value of the nickel that has been pulled down, 5.

7. To count 7, the next penny is pushed up and so on until you get to 10. At 10, the second nickel is pulled down and the pennies

are put back in their original place. Next, one penny in the second column is pushed up and the two nickels are put in their original places. This will read a 1 in the second column and a 0 in the first. Both of these positions mean 10.

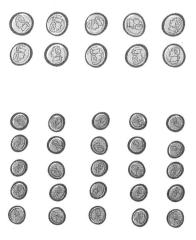

8. To count 11, the first penny in the second column stays up and the first penny in the first column is moved up.

9. This process continues using each column in order. You can actually use this five column counting board to count to 99,999!

Explanation

You should be able to keep track of your counting using the counting board you made in this activity. It will take practice until you can count very fast using it.

The difference between the counting board and an abacus is that the counting board was a piece of wood, stone, or metal with grooves or painted lines between which beads, pebbles, or metal disks were moved. The abacus is a device usually made of wood that has rods with freely sliding beads mounted on them. They both keep track of a count in the same way that you did in the activity.

The most common Chinese abacus has thirteen vertical wires with seven beads on each wire. The wire beads are in a rectangular frame. There is a horizontal divider within the frame so that the beads on

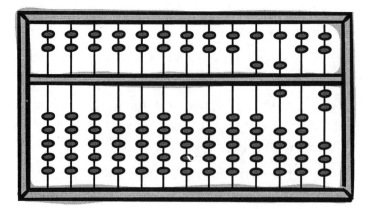

each wire are separated into a two-bead section above the divider (called the Heaven beads) and five beads below the divider (called the Earth beads).

You can read the count of the beads by simply looking at the number and position of the beads. The abacus on the previous page reads 5,602.

The abacus can add, subtract, multiply, and divide, as well as work with more difficult mathematical problems involving fractions and square roots. It was used through the Middle Ages and is still used today in many Asian countries.

Ancient Science in Action

The Chinese abacus was brought to other countries after its invention. There are also Japanese and Russian versions of similar bead-counting boards. Recent archaeological excavations have even found a type of Mesoamerican Aztec abacus from around 900 C.E. The counters were made from kernels of corn threaded through strings that were mounted on a wooden frame.

Earthquake!

Earthquakes have occurred all over the world throughout human history. Ancient people did not know what caused earthquakes, but they did know they could do great harm. The first instrument for monitoring earthquakes was invented by Zhang Heng in 130 C.E. His invention could detect an earthquake and indicate its direction from the capital of China, Luoyang. Try this activity to learn more about how Zhang Heng's invention worked.

Materials

2-by-4-by-12-inch (5-by-10-by-30 cm) piece of wood

tennis ball
table

Procedure

1. Stand the piece of wood on the table on one end.

2. Balance the tennis ball on top of the piece of wood.

3. Softly hit the table with your hand. What happens to the ball?

4. Hit the table hard with your fist. What happens to the ball this time?

More Fun Stuff to Do

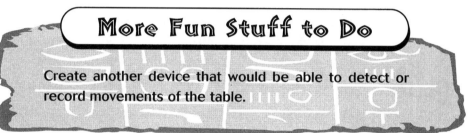

Create another device that would be able to detect or record movements of the table.

Explanation

When you hit the table lightly, the ball will remain balanced on the top of the piece of wood. But when you hit the table with your fist, the ball will fall off the board. (If you hit the table hard enough, the board itself will fall over.)

In this activity, you created an **earthquake** detector. Earthquakes occur when rock masses in the outer layer of the Earth suddenly move along ruptures in the Earth's surface called **faults.** The rock masses can move vertically, horizontally, or in combination. The location of the fault where there is the greatest amount of movement is called the **focus.** The **epicenter** is the point on the surface directly above the focus.

When the waves caused by an earthquake arrive at a point, they arrive in two stages. The first stage is the primary or P-waves. A P-wave causes the Earth to move back and forth so it quickly travels along the surface of the Earth. A short time later, secondary or

S-waves arrive. An S-wave causes the Earth to move up and down but travels more slowly than the P-wave.

Zhang Heng's original invention was a huge bronze pot that measured 6 feet (2 m) across. When an earthquake tremor hit the pot, it caused the release of a bronze ball from the mouth of one of six dragons that were carved along its outer surface. The ball that was released was farthest from the earthquake's epicenter. This notified the emperor of the direction of the disaster.

ANCIENT SCIENCE IN ACTION

Scientists today use a **seismograph** to monitor and measure an earthquake. A seismograph is a device that records the intensity and duration of an earthquake. It consists of a pen attached to a spring that writes on a revolving drum. When an earthquake arrives, the pen moves up and down on the drum, leaving a record of the earthquake. Although we have seismographs to monitor earthquakes after they arrive, we do not yet have a way to predict an earthquake.

7 SCIENCE FROM THE AMERICAS

Aztec, Mayan, and Native North American

While civilizations rose and fell in the Middle East, Africa, Europe, and Asia, independent civilizations developed in North and South America as well. Although we don't know exactly how or when these people arrived, most people believe they migrated from Asia around 12,000 B.C.E., crossing into Alaska from northeastern Russia across the Bering Strait when there was either a land bridge there or the oceans there were frozen. They continued their journey, eventually settling in various locations in North and South America.

For thousands of years, there was no contact between the peoples of North and South America and those on other continents. When the Spanish conquistadors first landed in this New World in Central and South America, they found gold and silver and marveled at the cities, temples, roads, and canals built by the native civilizations of the Mayans, the Aztecs, and the Incas. Ancient American civilizations explored many sciences, from astronomy and agriculture to mathematics and engineering.

To learn more about what early civilizations from the Americas discovered, try the activities in this chapter.

PROJECT 1

Sun Block

While some prehistoric peoples crossed into what is now Alaska and continued south to the United States and Mexico, some stayed in the far north. In about the year 1000, a warmer climate opened up the Beaufort Sea, and ancient people from Alaska followed the bowhead whale, a major food source, eastward. Some settled in Labrador and Greenland, beginning the Thule culture. Members of the Thule culture, who are the ancestors of the Inuit, developed a remarkable technology to deal with life in the Arctic. Try this activity to learn about one of the Thule devices used to protect their eyes from the sun.

Materials

large sheet of white paper   pencil
thin cardboard   scissors

Note: This activity should be done outside on a sunny day.

Procedure

1. Face the sun, holding the white paper horizontally in front of you, just below your chin. Look straight ahead. What do you notice? *(Note: Do not look directly at the sun.)*

2. Go back inside and place the cardboard on the table. Draw two ovals that join together to form the shape of sunglasses on the cardboard.

3. In the center of each oval, draw a horizontal slit that is 1 by ¼ inch (2.5 by .65 cm).

4. Use the scissors to cut out the sunglasses as well as the two slits.

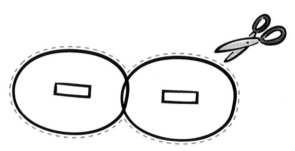

5. Go outside again and face the sun, holding the white paper horizontally in one hand in front of you, just below your chin. This time cover your eyes with your "sunglasses," holding them so you can look out through the slits. What do you notice this time?

Explanation

When you hold your "sunglasses" in front of your eyes, there will be less glare from the sun, and the sun will not seem as bright.

Our eyes adjust to the amount of light that enters them by opening or closing the **iris,** the round, pigmented membrane surrounding the pupil of the eye. Light that enters the eye is focused on the **retina,** the layer of cells on the back of the eye that are sensitive to light. When there is more light, the iris creates a smaller hole, and when there is less light, the iris creates a larger hole. If the iris lets too much light into the eye, it can damage the retina and cause the eye to go blind.

When there is snow on the ground, the light from the sun is not only entering your eye directly, it is also reflecting off the snow and entering your eyes indirectly. The iris cannot make the pupil small enough to keep this extra light from entering. If you were to look too long at the snow glare, you would eventually get snow blindness, in which you would be temporarily blinded and might have permanent eye damage. The slits in your "sunglasses" block this extra sunlight that reflects off the white paper in the same way that they would block some of the light that reflects off snow.

The Thule made snow goggles with slits in them similar to the goggles you made in this activity, to protect their eyes against snow blindness. The goggles were made of pieces of antler and held on the head with a cord made of sinew (animal tendon).

Ancient Science in Action

Besides snow goggles, the Thule (and the Inuit) developed other technologies to help them live in the frigid climate. Their homes were entered through a long tunnel, that dipped down at its center. This dip trapped cold air below the level of the house (cold air is more dense than warm air) and let Thule families rest comfortably on stone platforms covered with furs. They also invented the kayak, which they used to travel through the narrow waters between frozen blocks of ice.

PROJECT 2

Paddle Along

It is thought that the earliest travelers to North America came across the Bering Sea and dispersed to many places, forming different settlements. We now call all of these people Native Americans, but each group developed its own language, customs, and culture. Methods of transportation also varied, depending on the needs of the culture. One form of transportation developed by Native Americans from the Northeast and the Great Lakes regions is the birch bark canoe. The canoes made it easy to travel on narrow rivers, and they were light enough to carry over land. Try this activity to learn how to make a simple birch bark canoe.

Materials

6-by-8-inch (15-by-20-cm) piece of
   birch bark (available from craft
   stores)
water
pencil

scissors
large sewing needle
24-inch (60-cm) piece of dental
   floss
waterproof glue

Procedure

1. Soak the birch bark in water until it is flexible. The woody side should be intact.

2. Draw the pattern on the right on the birch bark.

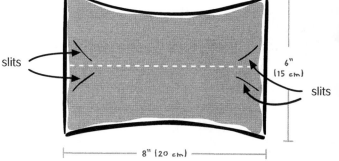

3. Use the scissors to cut out the birch bark pattern. Carefully cut the slits as shown.

4. Bend, but do not crease, the pattern in half lengthwise.

5. Pinch one end of the pattern together and fold up the small tab.

6. Thread the dental floss into the sewing needle.

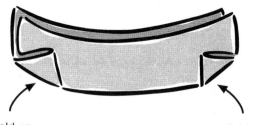

7. Begin sewing with a stitch that goes through the tab and both sides of the pattern. Continue stitching up and down the front edge of the canoe as shown in the diagram. When you finish sewing, knot the end of the dental floss and cut off the unused floss.

Stitch up

Stitch down

8. Repeat the sewing on the other end of the canoe.

9. Spread the center of the canoe to about 1 inch (2.5 cm) so it will float.

10. Fill any holes and cracks with waterproof glue.

11. Place your canoe in water. How does it float?

More Fun Stuff to Do

Try making the canoe out of other materials such as thin cardboard. How do these materials work?

Explanation

Your birch bark canoe should be able to float without sinking. Other materials will work for making the canoe if they are waterproof.

There are several types of birch trees. However, the best type of bark for usable items is the paper birch, sometimes called the white birch. The paper birch is found in many locations in North America. Removing the bark from a live birch can kill the tree if the inner bark is damaged. For this reason bark is usually gathered from fallen trees. Although this can be done at any time, the best time for gathering live birch bark is the late spring. If a tree has just fallen in the late spring, its outer bark will be the thickest and the dark inner bark is left on the tree. At this time, the bark is easily peeled off the fallen tree in bark sheets. These bark sheets were used for the outside of the birch bark canoes.

Birch bark was the perfect choice for canoes because it is lightweight and smooth as well as waterproof and rot resistant. The Native Americans would sew the joints of the canoe together using the root of the white pine and then further waterproof the canoe by applying hot pine or spruce sap.

ANCIENT SCIENCE IN ACTION

When explorers first visited North America, they quickly saw the versatility of the canoe. Fur traders often used canoes to travel far from civilization, usually up small rivers, and to haul the furs back. The fur trade in North America created such a demand for canoes, in fact, that the French set up the world's first canoe factory in Trois-Rivières, Quebec, around 1750. Many of the canoes that fur traders used were so big that they could carry a crew of 12 people and over 5,000 pounds (2,400 kg) of cargo.

PROJECT 3

Grow It

There are several plants that were first cultivated and grown in North America by the Mayans, Aztecs, and Native Americans. Both corn and beans are plants that were first grown in North America and were taken around the world by early explorers. And while many people think of Ireland as the birthplace of the potato, it was actually first grown by the Incas in the Andes Mountains of South America almost two thousand years ago. But the potato is different from many other vegetables. The potato doesn't grow on a bush, nor is it a root crop, like a carrot. So how does it grow? Try this activity to learn more about how potatoes grow.

Materials

small potato
paper bag
large clay pot
sandy soil

water
paper
pencil

Procedure

1. Cut the potato into several pieces so that each piece contains at least two or three potato eyes. A potato's eyes are the indentations on the surface of the potato. Don't peel the potato.

2. Lay the potato pieces in the sun for several days until the cut side of the potato dries out.

3. Place the potato in the paper bag and close it.

4. Set the potato in a dark place, such as in a closet. Check it every other day until you begin to see buds (the first plant shoots) start to grow out of the potato's "eyes."

5. Fill the clay pot half full of sandy soil.

6. Place the potato in the soil, then cover it with the remaining soil. The potato should be covered with about 1 inch (2.5 cm) of soil.

7. Add a small amount of water to the soil so it is moist.

8. Place the pot in a sunny location.

9. Keep the soil moist by placing a small amount of water in the pot each day. Be careful not to add too much water, so that the soil becomes soggy.

10. For the next two to four weeks, observe how the potato grows and record what you see.

11. After one month, remove the plant from the soil and look at the roots. What do you notice?

Explanation

The potato plant will begin to grow, with shoots visible through the soil in seven to ten days. The plant will continue to grow for the next few weeks, looking like a small bush. When you remove the potato plant from the soil after a month, you will notice long roots growing from the potato you planted with small round growths on the roots. These small round growths are called "tubers," and each will become a new potato.

Energy can be transformed from one form to another in many ways. One of the most common energy transformations that happens in nature is the conversion of light energy to chemical energy in plants. When plants are in sunlight, they undergo photosynthesis. In photosynthesis, the energy from the sun is used to cause chemical reactions that let the plants convert the chemicals carbon dioxide and water into glucose and oxygen. The plant then uses the glucose to grow taller and stronger, or the glucose is stored in the form of starch for later use. In the case of the potato plant, that starch is stored in the potato tuber.

But a potato is an unusual plant. When the potato or part of a potato is placed in the soil, a main shoot begins to grow within a week or so. This main shoot will break through the soil and become the green plant that you saw growing above the soil. Its leaves undergo photosynthesis and the plant grows further. At about the time the main shoot breaks through the surface, rhizomes arise from underground nodes on the main shoot. A **rhizome** is a creeping stem that grows horizontally a few inches (cm) under the ground. The rhizomes grow horizontally underground for 5 to 12 inches (7.5 to 30 cm), then thicken at the tip to form a tuber. This tuber will develop into a new potato.

There are pictures of a Peruvian potato god carved onto a leather plaque of the Nazca culture from around 400 C.E. Until 1500 C.E., the potato only grew in the Andes Mountains of Bolivia and Peru, in South America. The only people who ate potatoes were the Incas, a tribe of natives who lived there. When the Spanish conquistadors arrived in South America in the early 1500s, they didn't find the gold they were looking for, but they did find the potato and quickly developed an appetite for Peruvian potatoes. Potatoes were soon a standard supply item on all Spanish ships, and potato cultivation spread around the world. There are now hundreds of different varieties of potatoes.

ANCIENT SCIENCE IN ACTION

▲▲▲▲▲▲▲▲▲▲▲▲▲▲▲▲▲▲▲▲▲▲▲▲▲▲▲▲▲▲▲▲▲▲

One South American tribe, the Aymara Indians, who live above 10,000 feet (3,000 m) on the Titicaca Plateau in Peru, even developed a kind of freeze-drying process to preserve their potatoes. (In freeze drying, extreme cold is used to take the moisture out of food so it can be stored without refrigeration for long periods of time. When the food has to be eaten, water is added and the food is back to normal. Astronauts use freeze-dried food in space.)

The Aymara spread potatoes out on the ground on cold, frosty nights to freeze. They are then covered with straw during the day to keep them from thawing out. Each night they are uncovered, and the process continues. After several days and nights, the women and children trample the potatoes to get rid of the last moisture and wear away the potato's peel. The potatoes are then placed in a cold stream to wash out the bitter taste the potatoes naturally have. Finally, the potatoes are dried in the sun for about two weeks. Potatoes prepared this way can be stored for up to four years.

▲▲▲▲▲▲▲▲▲▲▲▲▲▲▲▲▲▲▲▲▲▲▲▲▲▲▲▲▲▲▲▲▲▲▲▲▲▲

PROJECT 4

North and North

The ancient Mayans knew that there was a difference between the Earth's magnetic north pole and the earth's geographic north pole. Their ancient city of Tulum, which dates to about 900 C.E., had towers that showed north, east, south, and west based on the rotation of the Earth. It also had a tower that was oriented to magnetic north. No one knows how they were able to discover this difference. Try this activity to discover the difference between the magnetic north pole and the geographic north pole of the Earth.

Materials

watch   magnetic compass
stick   protractor

Note: This activity should be done outside on a sunny day.

Procedure

1. Go outside at exactly 12:00 noon.

2. Poke the stick into the ground so that it stands vertically.

3. Note the direction in which the shadow points.

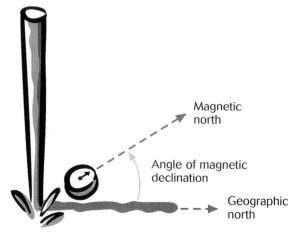

4. Hold the magnetic compass in front of you. In which direction does the needle point? Is it the same as the direction in which the shadow points?

5. Use the protractor to measure the angle between the direction in which the shadow points and the direction in which the magnetic compass needle points.

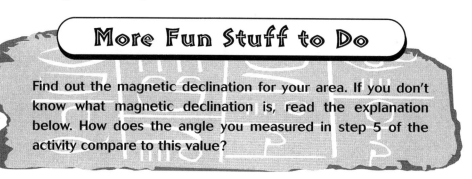

More Fun Stuff to Do

Find out the magnetic declination for your area. If you don't know what magnetic declination is, read the explanation below. How does the angle you measured in step 5 of the activity compare to this value?

Explanation

The magnetic compass points to magnetic north. The needle aligns itself in the same direction as the north magnetic pole of the Earth. The shadow points to true north, the direction of the north rotational pole. In most areas of the world, these will be slightly different directions. The measure of that difference should be approximately the magnetic declination for your area. Magnetic declination is the measure of the angle between the north magnetic pole and the north geographic pole.

Magnetic declination is different for each region of the country. It will range from 15 degrees west in the eastern United States to 15 degrees east in the western United States. In some areas of the Midwestern United States there is no magnetic declination, so magnetic compasses point to true north.

The Earth rotates on its axis once each day around an imaginary pole through its center. The place where this north rotational axis intersects with the surface of the Earth is called the **north geographic pole,** or sometimes true north. The **north magnetic pole** is located just north of Canada and west of Greenland.

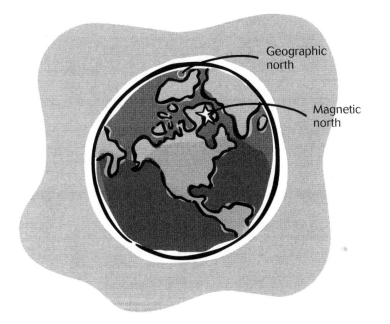

Geographic north

Magnetic north

Ancient Science in Action

When using a magnetic compass for navigation, you have to take the magnetic declination for the area into consideration in order to travel in the proper direction. For example, if you lived in the eastern United States and wanted to travel true north, you would actually need to travel about 15 degrees east of the direction that the magnetic compass told you was north.

Sun Track

Mayan astronomers watched the heavens, built observatories, and mapped the movements of the sun, moon, planets, and stars with remarkable accuracy. Over a thousand years ago they calculated the length of the solar year to be 365.2420 days. (Using modern technology, scientists today have determined the exact length of a solar year to be 365.2422 days—a difference of only a few seconds from the Mayan number.) Mayan astronomers also built special structures to track the sun. In the city of Tulum, they built a temple that had a small hole in its eastern wall and a special rock on the western wall. At sunrise on the first day of spring, light from the sun passed through the hole and illuminated the rock. In this way, the Mayans knew that it was time to start their planting season. Try the following activity to learn how to track the movement of the sun.

Materials

small mirror   masking tape
watch

Procedure

1. Place the mirror flat on the windowsill of a window that faces south, toward the sun. The mirror should be positioned so that the sun will reflect off it, leaving a reflected spot on a wall on the opposite side of the room.

2. At exactly 12:00 noon, place a small piece of tape on the wall in the center of the reflected spot.

3. At 15-minute intervals, place other small pieces of tape in the center of the reflection. After 60 minutes, what do you notice?

4. At exactly 12:00 noon the next day, place a small piece of tape on the wall in the center of the reflection.

5. Place a small piece of tape on the wall in the center of the reflection each day at exactly 12:00 noon for the next two weeks. What do you notice?

Explanation

When you place a piece of tape in the center of the reflection at fifteen-minute intervals, the pieces of tape show that the reflection moves over time. If you place a piece of tape in the center of the reflection at the same time every day, you will notice that the reflection is moving each day as well.

The movement of the reflection shows the motion of the Earth. The reflection moves throughout the day as the Earth turns on its axis, which makes the sun appear to move across the sky. The reflection moves from day to day because the Earth orbits the sun. If you tracked the movement of the sun's reflection at the same time each day for a year, you would return to the original spot in exactly one year.

ANCIENT SCIENCE IN ACTION

The Mayans used their observations of the sun to create a 365-day solar calendar. Actually, they had two calendars: a 260-day sacred year used for religious purposes and the 365-day solar year for planting. Every 52 years the two calendars came together and began again at the same moment. The Mayan 365-day calendar was different from our calendar. Instead of 12 months of 28 to 31 days, it had 18 months of 20 days each, with an extra 5-day period called Uayeb at the end of the year. The Mayans knew that this "Vague Year" did not exactly equal a solar year, but the Uayeb could be extended to keep their planting calendar and the solar year in step.

Other ancient civilizations had their own calendars. The ancient Romans borrowed the Greek lunar calendar, which divided the year into 10 months. In the 7th century B.C.E., the Roman emperor Numa Pompilius added 2 months (January and February) to bring the calendar in line with the solar year of 365 days. But the addition of the extra months did not fix the Roman calendar for long. The calendar was off by a day every 4 years, and over time the calendar year slowly lost pace with the seasons of the year as winter began to come when the calendar said it should be fall, and summer came when the calendar said it was spring. To correct this, the Roman emperor Julius Caesar, who also named the month of July after himself, corrected the solar year to $365\frac{1}{4}$ days by adding a leap year, which added an extra day every four years. To get the calendar back in line with the seasons, Julius Caesar added 80 days to one year. So the year 46 B.C.E. had 445 days and became known as *ultimus annus confusionis,* the last year of confusion.

Glossary

alloy   A mixture of metals.

Archimedes' principle   A scientific principle that states that an immersed object is buoyed up by a force equal to the weight of the fluid it displaces.

archaeologist   A scientist who studies the life and culture of past peoples.

artifact   Any object made by humans, such as primitive tools, weapons, cooking pots, or works of art.

astronomy   The study of the sun and stars.

Bernoulli's principle   A scientific principle that states that when air flows, its pressure decreases as its speed increases.

cell wall   A special material that surrounds plant cells.

chemical reaction   A change in matter in which substances break apart to produce one or more new substances.

chemistry   The science that investigates matter.

city-state   A state made up of an independent city and the surrounding territory directly controlled by it.

concrete   A hard building material made by mixing cement with sand and water. The concrete can be made stronger by adding rock pieces, called aggregate.

crystal   A chemical compound that forms a solid in a specific pattern that repeats regularly in all directions.

earthquakes   The sudden movement of the outer layer of the Earth.

electrum   A natural alloy (mixture) of gold and silver.

epicenter   The point on the surface directly above the focus.

faults   Ruptures in the Earth's surface.

friction   The force that opposes motion.

focus   The location of the fault where there is the greatest amount of movement.

fossil   Bones that have been turned to stone.

hieroglyphic   An ancient Egyptian form of writing in which a picture or symbol is used to represent a word, symbol, or sound.

hydroelectricity   The electrical energy generated from the gravitational energy of falling water.

hydrophilic   The part of a molecule that is attracted to water.

hydrophobic   The part of a molecule that repels water.

hypothesis   An educated guess about the results of an experiment to be performed.

iris   The round, pigmented membrane surrounding the pupil of the eye.

incident ray   Light that travels from an object to a mirror.

law of reflection   A scientific principle in optics that states that the measure of the angle of the reflected ray and the mirror and the measure of the angle of the incident ray and the mirror are always equal.

lens   A piece of glass or other transparent substance with a curved surface that refracts or bends and brings together rays of light passing through it.

lever   A simple machine made of a rigid board or bar that is supported at a fixed point called a fulcrum.

magnetic declination   The measure of the angle between the north magnetic pole and the north geographic pole.

magnetism   An invisible force that attracts certain metals to magnets.

mechanical advantage   The amount by which a machine can multiply a force.

medicine   The science of diagnosing, treating, and preventing disease and preserving health.

navigate   To steer a course.

north geographic pole   The place where the north rotational axis intersects with the surface of the Earth.

north magnetic pole   The place located below the surface of the Earth just north of Canada and west of Greenland that magnetic compasses point to.

octave   The eight notes that make a musical scale.

optics   The field of physics that studies the properties of light.

parabolic reflectors   A curved mirror that has the ability to take light rays that strike them and make them travel out in one direction.

percussion instrument   An instrument that makes a sound when hitting it causes the instrument to vibrate.

118

photosynthesis A chemical reaction in plants where energy from the sun is used to bond carbon, hydrogen, and oxygen atoms into glucose, which is used by other organisms as their main food energy source.

pitch The relative highness or lowness of a sound.

reflected Bounced.

reflected ray The light from an object after it reflects off a mirror and travels in a straight line to your eye.

refract The bending of a light path as it travels from one transparent material to another.

reservoir A large storage lake behind a dam.

retina The layer of cells on the back of the eye that are sensitive to light.

rhizome A creeping stem that grows horizontally a few inches (cm) under the ground.

scientific method The process used to investigate a scientific question that involves forming a hypothesis, testing the hypothesis with an experiment, analyzing the results, and drawing a conclusion.

seismograph A device that records the intensity and duration of an earthquake.

static electricity Electricity that does not flow.

trigonometry The study of the relationship between the sides and angles of triangles.

turbine A special kind of water wheel used in a hydroelectric plant.

wind instrument An instrument that makes a sound when you blow air into it, causing the air inside it to vibrate.

Index